FOR THE RECORD
ISRAEL AND THE PALESTINIANS
What the Media Aren't Telling You

Alan B. Katz

NEW YORK ◆ JERUSALEM ◆ LONDON

For the Record:
What the Media Aren't Telling You
Published by Devora Publishing Company
Text Copyright © 2008 *Alan B. Katz. All rights reserved.*

Portions of this book were first published in 2007 under the former title, FIGHTING BACK

Cover Design: Benjie Herskowitz
Typesetting & Book Design: Koren Publishing Services
Editor: Ilan Chaim
Editorial & Production Manager: Daniella Barak

No part of this book may be used or reproduced or transmitted in any form or by any means, electronic or mechanical, including photocopying, recording, or by any information storage and retrieval system, without written permission from the publisher.

Hard Cover ISBN: 978-1-932687-73-6

E-MAIL: sales@devorapublishing.com
WEB SITE: www.devorapublishing.com

Printed in the United States of America

This book is dedicated to the memories of my father, Howard Katz, *z"l*, and my grandfather, Philip Adler, *z"l*, whose love, wisdom and kindness were plentiful, and of whom it may be said that they were proud sons of Abraham. Their lives were well and truly a blessing.

CONTENTS

Author's Note · vi
Acknowledgments · vii
Abbreviations · viii
Preface · ix
Letters · 1
Appendix of Essays · 217
    1. Self-Defense – Both a Sword and a Shield (1982) · 217
    2. Hafez Letter to *The New York Times* (1986) · 222
    3. The Middle East "Peace" Conference (1991) · 226
    4. What You Wish For (2005) · 229
    5. Old Wine in Old Bottles (2005) · 233
    6. Judenrein in the Promised Land (2008) · 239

AUTHOR'S NOTE

There are many excellent sites on the Internet which expose media misinformation and anti-Israel bias. Primary among them are the Committee for Accuracy in Middle East Reporting in America (camera.org) and Honest Reporting (honestreporting.com). Both sites provide current information on media malfeasance and bias, identify the offending media and refer us to accurate sources of information. Additionally, One Family Fund (www.onefamilyfund.org) is an extra-ordinary organization dedicated to assisting individuals and families who are victims of terrorist attacks. They are all worthy of our financial support.

ACKNOWLEDGMENTS

Excerpt from "Always, Darkness Visible" first published in the New York Times Op-Ed ©1981 by Aharon Appelfeld, permission of the Wylie Agency.

Many "Letters" appeared in the on-line Jerusalem Post and the print edition of the International Jerusalem Post, permission to reprint same here is most gratefully acknowledged.

Many thanks to my publisher, Yaacov Peterseil, my editor, Ilan Chaim, and Daniella S. Barak, my production manager, for their patience and professional guidance.

Abbreviations

EU	European Union
IAF	Israel Air Force
IDF	Israel Defense Forces
ICJ	International Court of Justice
IJP	International Jerusalem Post
JP	*The Jerusalem Post*
NYT	*The New York Times*
PA	Palestinian Authority
PLO	Palestine Liberation Organization
UNIFIL	United Nations Interim Force in Lebanon
WSJ	*The Wall Street Journal*

PREFACE

Mark Twain, the great American writer and chronicler of human frailties, once observed, "If you don't read the newspapers, you are uninformed. If you do read the newspapers, you are misinformed."

Nowhere is the truth of Twain's observation more evident than in the reporting on the Middle East. Read the headlines. Listen to the news. "Israel Humiliates Palestinians." "Israeli Check-Points Prevent Palestinians From Getting to Work." "Israel Closes Gaza Crossing as Unemployment Escalates." "Israel Attacks Lebanon With Excessive Force. Civilian Casualties Mount." For too long the media have treated Israel like their personal piñata; skewed reporting and putting a particular "spin" on the news in the Middle East have become common. Subtle falsehoods, doctored photographs and blood libels were all part of the mechanism for blaming the Israelis for everything in the Middle East, from the Palestinian refugee situation to the price of oil and the US-Iraq war.

There is little effort to be fair and even-handed. The Arab/Palestinian viewpoint is invariably expressed out of context or in a vacuum. Newspapers and news services such as *The New York*

Times and Reuters, and television networks such as ABC and the BBC, are often the greatest offenders. You cannot even trust your eyes. As Palestinian police, soldiers and kids stage phony firefights and rioting, French cameras roll as if on cue. These staged scenes are then broadcast on French television as "news."

The case of Muhammad al-Dura is one of the most disturbing examples of the media fabricating the news, and always at the expense of the Israelis. This blood libel stirred up anti-Israel passions around the world. In the afternoon of September 30, 2000, at the beginning of the so-called al-Aksa intifada, 12-year-old al-Dura and his father were walking to their Gaza home when they were caught in the cross-fire between the IDF and Palestinian snipers. The older al-Dura tried to shield his son, but young Muhammad was shot. The Palestinian television crew for France 2 was on the scene filming. Later that day, a France 2 reporter – who was not present that afternoon – was shown the film and, based on what he was told, narrated the death of Muhammad al-Dura by the Israelis.

Palestinian television edited the film and pictures of an Israeli soldier shooting were spliced into the original footage, creating the false impression that the IDF shot the boy. Headlines screamed: "Israeli Occupation Forces Kill Palestinian Child in Cold Blood".

The picture of Muhammad and his father huddled against a wall was flashed across the world and in record time al-Dura was the poster boy for Israeli murder and the entire "occupation." Al-Dura's name and picture were used by incensed Muslims across the Middle East and Europe as an excuse for rioting and outright murder. Al-Dura was mentioned during the decapitation of *Wall Street Journal* reporter Daniel Pearl. He was again invoked when Muslims rioted across Europe in response to newspaper cartoons depicting Islamic Prophet Muhammad with a missile in his turban. And al-Dura was invoked once again in the savage murder in Amsterdam of filmmaker Theo Van Gogh.

The problem is that al-Dura was not killed by the IDF. In a French courtroom this year a French ballistics expert, whose credentials have been accepted for 20 years, testified that given the locations of the boy, the IDF soldiers and the Palestinians, it was impossible for the boy to have been shot by the soldiers. Rather, young al-Dura was killed by Palestinian snipers. Moreover, the film shown in a French court showed al-Dura moving and waving moments *after* he was declared by the reporter to have been shot dead. On May 21, 2008, a French appeals court held that Jewish activist Philippe Karsenty did not libel France 2 and its reporters when he charged that the film was a staged hoax.

Among the many questions that arise out of the al-Dura incident are these: What happens to the law when the media lie? What happens to history when the media lie?

In another stunning example of media bias, on September 30, 2000, *The New York Times* printed a photograph purporting to show a bloodied Palestinian youth cowering in front of an Israeli policeman holding a baton. In fact, the youth was an American yeshiva student who had been pulled from a taxi and beaten and stabbed by Palestinians. Moreover, the accompanying text erroneously stated that the assault had occurred on the Temple Mount, whereas the assault occurred in the Arab neighborhood of Wadi al Joz. And the policeman was there to protect him. After the *Times* printed an insubstantial "correction," public outcry compelled the *Times* to rerun the photo and tell the true story of how the Jewish American student was almost murdered by the Palestinians.

* * *

Moreover, the pro-Palestinian spin has bastardized our language, descending into Orwellian *Newspeak* where "Good is Bad," "Bad is Good," "War is Peace" and "Peace is War." Israel is frequently identified as an "apartheid" state. This is more than just spinning words. It is an outright lie. To the contrary, it was the Palestinians who demanded, and obtained, the removal of all Jews from Gaza. Not one country – not even the United States – uttered so much as a word of protest when the Palestinians demanded the ethnic cleansing of Gaza. Israel, alone among all Middle East nations, has religious diversity among its citizenry and legislature. Arabs make up nearly 20 percent of Israel's citizens and have seats in the Knesset, Israel's legislature, as well as a portfolio in the Prime Minister's Cabinet. Not even in those Arab countries that have a peace treaty with Israel is a Jew permitted to so much as own land or vote. Yet former President Jimmy Carter travels the world promoting his own epistle to mendacity, the cover of which declares an apartheid Israel

Palestinians who shoot at Israelis or plant roadside bombs, and teenagers who blow themselves up in the middle of a café or discotheque are identified as "militants" or even just "gunmen." The word "terrorist" is not used to describe these acts of cold-blooded murder. (Nevertheless, when American immigrant Baruch Goldstein murdered 29 Muslim worshipers in a mosque in Hebron in 1994, the Israelis immediately branded him a terrorist.)

Even when a pregnant Israeli mother and her four young daughters were murdered in their car, the media blamed the victims, saying they shouldn't have been where they were – which was on a public road approaching their community in the middle of the day.

It was bad enough that Israeli children were being murdered, but the media always seemed to pluck a string from the Palestinian violin. Someone had to take on the media. I decided not to "let it go" and watch the media portray the Israelis as heartless monsters. I could think of six million reasons.

I wrote to newspapers and television stations and called them on their anti-Israel – and sometimes anti-Semitic – articles and programs. Occasionally, a newspaper would print a letter. Television stations and others also occasionally responded in writing, invariably trying to explain away irresponsible journalism.

* * *

There has been an alarming increase in global anti-Semitism. Sweden pulls out of an international air show upon learning that

Israel and the Palestinians – What the Media Aren't Telling You

the Israel Air Force will participate. A Norwegian school tells a Christian teacher that he can't wear a ½-inch Star of David around his neck in school as it might inflame the Arab students. Paris tells its Jewish students that to avoid being assaulted, they should not wear yarmulkes in public. And in Britain, isolating Israel has taken the form of educators being urged to boycott not only Israel's universities and conferences, but also Israeli scholars and students who refused to disavow their government's "apartheid" policies. Even the Oxford debating society recently argued whether Israel should exist! Violent acts of anti-Semitism – from physical attacks on Jewish youths to desecration of Jewish schools and cemeteries – have been on the rise throughout Europe.

Four years ago a poll from the EU was released in which it was revealed that 75% of Europeans polled believed Israel to be the single greatest threat to world peace. This in a world of Darfur, Rwanda, Iran's lunatic leader hell-bent on obtaining nuclear weapons in order to "wipe Israel off the face of the Earth," Muslim terror groups supported by the Arabs, nuclear weapons in the hands of a quasi-rational North Korean leader and Islamist extremists who riot and kill over a cartoon. To point the finger at Israel smacked of anti-Semitism.

I am not remonstrating with people who in good faith disagree with Israel's policies. I am referring to people who hold Israel to a different standard of morality; people who stand mute when Palestinian terrorists murder Israeli children and then object when Israel destroys the house of the suicide bomber – all the while spilling not one drop of Palestinian blood. I am speaking of people who would deny Israel her natural right to self-defense.

Lastly, we find this prejudice even in America. Mr. Carter is not alone. Recently, the then-head of the Kennedy School at Harvard and his colleague at the University of Chicago published a book that blames the US-Iraq war on the Jewish-American lobby, as if less than 2 percent of our population could ever force this country to go to war. Hell, we could not even persuade F.D.R. to save the Jews on the *St. Louis*.

For the Record

We are under attack to an extent unseen since the Second World War. Israel will soon face an existential threat from Iran as America and the nations of Europe watch Iran's annihilator president rush head-on to precipitate Armageddon, certain that it will mark the end of the Jewish people and the beginning of international Islamic rule.

I will not try to explain anti-Semitism.

I do not understand that particular pathology. In our own sometimes irrational desire to be accepted around the world, rather than confronting anti-Semitism, we often "let it go" for fear of creating a scene. There are not enough of us left anymore to just let it go. There is too much hatred in the world and it well serves a free society to engage bigotry everywhere.

Jewish citizens around the world often try to be assimilated into society as though being Jewish were a source of disgrace. Hitler proved that we cannot be "Jewish in our homes and German outside." But in America, where Irish, Hispanic and Italian Americans, among others, proudly and rightly preserve their ethnic cultures, so too must it be acceptable for us to be both Americans and Jewish. It is not a question of loyalty, but heritage.

We cannot wait for God to "take us out of Egypt" again; or for the rest of the world to accept us; or to rely on others to protect Israeli children, homes and borders. It is up to us now to pick up from where the Jews of Masada, Bar Kochba and the brave men of the IDF and the IAF who flew to Entebbe and Osirak left off. I was particularly moved by these words from a Holocaust survivor:

> "This is not a story with a happy ending. A doctor who survived, from a religious background, who sailed to Israel with us in June 1946, told us: 'We didn't see God when we expected him, so we have no choice but to do what he was supposed to do: we will protect the weak, we will love, we will comfort. From now on, the responsibility is all ours.'"

("Always, Darkness Visible," by Aharon Appelfeld, *New York Times*, Op-Ed, January 27, 2005, p. A25.)

It is my hope – indeed, the very purpose of putting these letters together – that this book will show the toll this conflict has taken on the Israelis, clear the record for Israel and stand up to the media for trying to put an Israeli face on death and hatred.

What is happening in Israel, Gaza and Judea and Samaria is gut-wrenching. And there is no end in sight. But, before we can solve issues, it is necessary to have an accurate and clear command of the facts.

A.B.K.
Melville, New York

Israel and the Palestinians – What the Media Aren't Telling You

March 21, 1997

Mr. Anthony Lewis
The New York Times

Dear Mr. Lewis,

    I was rather bewildered by your attempt to rationalize the Jordanian murder last week of seven Israeli schoolgirls .... Curiously, your own article of March 14 provided the bill of particulars by which we may conclude that the current atmosphere of Palestinian terrorism is condoned – we may even say invited.

    Over a disagreement in policy – remarkably, the right of Jews to live in Israel's capital – the Arab leaders, by your own account, told the Israelis that there would be violence. Mubarak, Hussein and Arafat called for the violence and then you excuse these murders because the Israelis were forewarned. You ask, "Does Mr. Netanyahu understand how dangerous the situation is?" I question whether you understand why the situation is so dangerous.

    You should not underestimate how the media's inexhaustible obsequiousness to the Palestinians feeds and gives comfort to their inexhaustible hatred of the Jews. People such as yourself argue without rationale that it was a reckless provocation for Israel to build homes for Jews in Israel's capital, thus resulting in the unspeakable murders you seemingly excuse. How can you morally or politically explain away the murder of children.

    You no doubt know of today's bombing by Palestinian terrorists in Tel Aviv. Did you despair for the suicide bomber? Will you write yet another column blaming Israel for this too? How many more Jewish bodies do you need to see blown apart before you figure out the distinction between predator and victim? Three days ago, the Palestinians started moving people out of their hospitals. Why? To make room for their casualties as they were preparing to respond to their leaders' exhortations to violence over Har Homa. The Palestinians will continue this war – and make no mistake that this is a war to the death – for their state and the destruction of Israel.

If Israel does not respond to these events, the Likud government will have abandoned its first obligation, i.e., to protect its citizens. When Israel does respond, you will no doubt pen another condemnation of Israeli intransigence.

As I watched a six-month-old infant being carried from the site of today's blast, I thought of your article. You ask if the Israelis know what they were doing to the "peace process." Seven dead children, Mr. Lewis. Some peace process.

On August 6, 2001, the Jerusalem Post published a letter about the intifada which referred to the movie The Godfather – Part II, *quoting Michael Corleone in pre-Castro Havana: The rebels can win because they're willing to die.*

August 6, 2001

To the Editor (JP):

So now, based on Michael Corleone's wisdom in *The Godfather, Part II*, you conclude that the Palestinians can win because they are willing to die in their war against Israel?

If the movies are to be your source of military philosophy, I personally prefer the opening scene in the movie *Patton* in which the general reminds his troops that "No bastard ever won a war by dying for his country. He won it by making the *other* poor dumb bastard die for *his* country."

For the Record

November 13, 2001

To the Editor (NYT):

The letter of Hesham El Nakib, press counselor to the Egyptian Embassy in Washington ("Arabs Reject Terror," November 9) plays upon a duplicity all too common in the Arab world, i.e., that they speak with two voices: one for the Arabs and another for America and Europe. Thus, although Arafat assures the Western media that he desires peace, this past April he spoke at a conference in Iran in which he stated that his people would fight the Israelis until Jewish blood flowed throughout the land.

For his part, Mr. El Nakib states: "In reality, Arab leaders and citizens have spoken out on numerous occasions condemning the heinous acts of terror perpetrated against America." Nor, he urges, should Americans fail to acknowledge the "principled stand that the Arabs and Egypt have taken against terrorism." How have the Egyptian leaders responded to America's ordeal?

> "Although some regretted the killing of innocent Americans in Washington and New York, most of [our] people derived satisfaction.... There was nearly an Egyptian consensus on the matter, except for a few ministers who, in their hypocrisy, rushed to the American Embassy to ostentatiously offer their condolences."

That from the Egyptian government-sponsored newspaper *Al Ahkbar* this past September 25.

The Egyptian newspaper *Al-Arabi* on September 16 offered further evidence of what Mr. El Nakib called Egypt's "principled stand against terrorism."

> "In all honesty, and without beating around the bush: I am happy about [what happened to] America; I am happy about the great number of American dead."

Israel and the Palestinians – What the Media Aren't Telling You

This from *Al-Usbu' Al Adabi*, an Egyptian/pan-Arab newspaper, on September 17: "Bush, drink from the bitter cup of the blood of your people, so that you will know that Allah is just!"

The Egyptian people expressed their "condemn[ation] of the heinous acts of terror perpetrated against America," with these comforting words from *Al Maydan*, an independent Egyptian newspaper, on September 24:

> "Millions across the world shouted in joy: America was hit! This expressed the sentiments of millions across the world, whom the American master had treated with tyranny, arrogance, bullying, conceit, deceit, and bad taste – like every bully whom no one has yet put in his place."

Whom does Mr. El Nakib think he is kidding? The Arab leaders tell their people what is in their hearts, and then tell Americans and Europeans what we want to hear. I don't blame the Arabs for their hypocrisy so much as I do the West for winking at it. So much for Egypt's ecumenical receipt of billions of US dollars in foreign aid.

For the Record

March 25, 1992

To the Editor (NYT):

Re: "Denied a State for Decades," Arafat, it now appears, carries some serious luggage – Iran. With a radical, fundamentalist, Muslim Palestine along Israel's border, the destabilization of the Middle East will make Hitler's march into Poland look like a cocktail party. In the past, Israel was told to choose between suicide and murder. With the demand for a Palestinian/Iranian state on its border, it appears that Israel is urged to suffer both fates.

To Shimon Peres and other appeasers who thought the Palestinians were only a political problem to be solved with boundaries, you had to know that it would come to this when Arafat got away with the cold-blooded murder of our children in Ma'alot, Jerusalem, Tel Aviv and Afula, to name just a few cities.

The first time Peres and the other appeasers let Palestinians get away with the murder of Jewish children, we knew that it would come to this. The Security Council's declaration in favor of a Palestinian state has the same persuasive ring as *Arbeit Macht Frei*.

Arafat is the Trojan horse, and inside are the terrorists and Islamic fundamentalists who crave the death of Israel. This is pure, unadulterated hatred and they have already come after us. America now has "skin in the game" and she can no longer be neutral. This is a time for free men to stand up, arm in arm, back to back, shoulder to shoulder.

This letter followed a meeting between Arafat and Secretary of State Colin Powell.

April 14, 2002

To the Editor (NYT)

It is virtually incomprehensible – other than in terms of oil – why Secretary Powell visited Arafat yesterday. Had even one of Arafat's many declarations against violence been bona fide, we would not have witnessed the ongoing massacres of Israeli women and children since the Oslo Accords.

This country launched a war against Afghanistan in response to a single – albeit horrific – morning of terror. Yet Israel is to be denied the right to hunt down the proponents and practitioners of this raging war against its civilians. We witness what George Will properly called our nation's "inexhaustible obsequiousness" toward the Arabs.

Powell's appeasement of Arafat and the Arabs is doomed to failure. With every utterance to Israel to back down, we encourage the Palestinians to escalate the carnage.

Churchill well understood this when, upon Chamberlain's return to England in 1938, the great man called the Munich agreement "an unmitigated disaster." Instead of having to conquer Czechoslovakia, Hitler was content to have it served up to him on a plate. So, it seems, will it be with Gaza and the West Bank.

For the Record

May 3, 2002

To the Editor (NYT):

Your editorial ("Now that Arafat is Free," May 3) was more interesting for what it concealed than for what it revealed. Implicit in the piece was disapproval of Israel's actions in principle. By referring to "a toxic occupation" and "the Israeli offensive," the *Times* exhibits a failure to grasp evenly the origins and course of this conflict.

Israel's offensive was necessitated by the relentless assault of suicide bombers. Indeed, its actions were defensive. And by referring to an "occupation" you fail to distinguish between the fire and the firemen.

Two years ago, Arafat was offered almost every territory he had demanded of the Israelis. The Palestinian response to Israel's unprecedented offer was war, the second intifada.

May 29, 2002

To the Editor (Newsday):

In the last three days, we have suffered two Palestinian suicide bombings. Monday, a grandmother and her 15-month-old grandchild were killed in Petah Tikva.

Today, another suicide bomber took the lives of three yeshiva boys. A horrible chill went through me when it was reported that the murderer's father wished his son had been carrying a nuclear bomb! Has all sanity and love of one's child completely left the Palestinians? How, in the name of all that is sacred, can a Palestinian mother – *any* mother – declare, as one recently did, that she would give the lives of all five of her children to get her land back from the Jews?

All of which leads me to believe that in the foreseeable future – and possibly in my lifetime – the Palestinians will never live in peace with Israel. Perhaps the politics of the Middle East was foreseen centuries ago when Shakespeare wrote in *Richard III* "despair and die."

For the Record

August 5, 2002

To the Editor (Newsday):

Your coverage of the death of nine Israelis on a public bus near Safed, although informative, lacked one vital and revealing perspective – the Palestinian response to this act of murder. Over 4,000 Palestinians celebrated the massacre, passed out candy, shot rifles into the air, and cheered a Hamas member who told the crowd that the Jews had "better prepare more body bags."

This, then, is the primary reason there will never be peace in the region: the Palestinians hate the Jews more than they cherish life, even the lives of their children. How can anyone make peace with people who celebrate the murder of children and who encourage their own children to commit suicide? Such naked hatred negates any possibility of reconciliation. More than their own state – which Barak handed them on a silver plate two years ago – the Palestinians fanatically desire the death of the entire Jewish population.

Israel and the Palestinians – What the Media Aren't Telling You

September 25, 2002

Letters to the Editor (NYT):

Professors Cavanaugh and Spelke's letter reveals that very prejudice and hypocrisy of which Harvard President Lawrence Summers spoke last week. Israel is chastised for defending its citizens as though those actions occur in a vacuum. Israel responds to Palestinian terrorism aimed almost always against Israel's civilians and all too frequently against her children, as occurred at a schoolhouse in Ma'alot and the Dolphinarium discotheque in Tel Aviv. Are they unaware of these and so many other calculated atrocities committed by the Palestinians in the name of "peace?"

Profs. Cavanaugh and Spelke demand an end to "the occupation" in the name of peace. What kind of peace? Media darling Hanan Ashwari states that the Palestinians should have all of Israel, while massive armaments are being imported into the West Bank and children are taught to kill Jews. Not in 54 years, including the 19 years that Jordan controlled the West Bank, can they point to even one rally for peace among the Palestinians. Yet the professors continue to see this conflict solely through the eyes of the Palestinians. One must question their good faith and ask "Why?"

Moreover, Profs. Cavanaugh and Spelke fail to place Israel's conduct in context. I would be interested to know whether they support divestment against Saudi Arabia, Egypt, Jordan or Syria, each of which harbors and/or directly supports Hizbullah, Islamic Jihad, Hamas and the Palestinian suicide bombers. Perhaps the professors can explain why they stood mute when three million Palestinians cheered and celebrated on September 11.

For the Record

June 11, 2003

Letters to the Editor (NYT):

Your editorial "Unwelcome Surprise" illustrates the refusal to distinguish between hope and reality. As you acknowledge, between the hope for peace and the reality of Arab politics lie the bodies of men, women and children; with the Israelis trying on the one hand to stop the violence, and the Palestinians on the other, with their deeply imbedded hatred, doing everything in their power to escalate it.

It is one thing to acknowledge Israel's right to defend herself and quite another to deny her right to target those who oil the machinery of murder. Only days ago, Hamas leader Rantisi declared Abbas *persona non grata* and reiterated Hamas's dedication to the destruction of Israel. Forty-eight hours later, in an uncommon show of cooperation, Hamas joined forces with Islamic Jihad and Al Aksa Martyrs Brigade and, disguised in IDF uniforms, murdered five Israelis.

To opine that Israel's response was "a clear escalation" that "undercuts the credibility of the new Palestinian prime minister" completely misses the point and is factually inaccurate. It was not the Israeli response that undercut Abbas. Rather, it was the terrorists' coordinated, joint attack and murder of the five Israelis which sent the message hot on the heals of Aqaba that Abbas does not represent the Palestinians, that they would not even meet with him, that there would be no negotiated cease-fire (much less disarmament) and no peace for Israel. Abbas is now standing alone in the storm still trembling in the fear that Arafat will fire him – unless, of course, terrorists murder him as they did Sadat and Bashir Gamayel. To urge that Abbas be given further opportunities to end violence against Israel is an exercise in self-deception. Abbas lacks the will, the muscle and the popular support.

Penultimately, you correctly point out that the cycle of violence begins with the Palestinians. It is, therefore, only from the Palestinian people that peace may emanate. Unfortunately, they do not want peace. Hundreds of millions of dollars have flowed into the Palestinian Authority, yet the squalid refugee camps under UN supervision for over half a century still stand. When Iraqi Scud missiles hit Tel Aviv in 1991, the Palestinians stood on their roof-tops and cheered. When two Israeli reservists took a wrong turn into Ramallah, they were beaten to death in the Palestinian police station; one of the murderers proudly showing his bloody hands to eager cameramen. And when America and England recently captured Iraq, it was the Palestinians who marched with placards urging "Beloved Saddam, Destroy Tel Aviv."

Finally, where is a Palestinian peace movement? Why aren't Palestinian mothers demonstrating in front of Arafat's offices demanding an end to the death of their children instead of declaring, as one Palestinian father did, that he was only sorry that his son, dead in a suicide bombing, did not carry a nuclear bomb. Golda Meir was right when she said that there will be no peace as long as the Arabs hate the Jews more than they love their children. So far, there is no evidence to the contrary.

Oxfam International is an organization which, according to its Web site, "works with communities, allies and partner organizations, undertaking long-term development, emergency work, research and campaigning for a fairer world." Its Belgian office published a call on its Internet web site for a ban on all Israeli products coming from the West Bank.

To Oxfam International:

July 18, 2003

Gentlemen:

Your explanation of the Belgian Web site's call for a ban on Israeli products is essentially a distinction without a difference. It is anti-Israel and anti-Jewish, because it distorts facts and singles out the Israeli people on a basis not applied to any other nation.

You are incorrect in stating that the West Bank is "Israeli occupied." When did this occupation commence and against whom is it directed? If the alleged occupation is against the non-Jewish inhabitants of the West Bank, then why wasn't Jordanian control from 1948 to 1967 also an occupation? The real answer is because Jordan was created out of 88 % of pre-WWII Palestine and the Palestinian Arabs refused to share the other 12 % with the Palestinian Jews.

Why did the Israeli army enter the West Bank? Because Jordan, which occupied it, attacked Israel from there in the 1967 Six Day War. Since then the Palestinians have been killing Jews and no one has done anything to stop it except the Israeli army. That remains, to this day, the underlying problem in the West Bank and, therefore, the reason for the presence of Israeli troops. Compel the Arabs to stop killing Jews and the Israeli army will withdraw. It's that easy.

Oxfam's position is anti-Israeli, because it seeks to punish the Israelis for doing something that every other nation has the right to do – that is, defend its citizens. Why is it that self-defense is available to all but the Jewish state? Kindly explain that.

Israel and the Palestinians – What the Media Aren't Telling You

A similar argument against Oxfam's boycott is its hypocrisy. Even assuming, merely for the sake of argument, that Israel is an occupying force, how does Oxfam categorize the Syrian presence in Lebanon? Before the fall of communism, can you recall a single instance in which Poland was described as "Soviet-occupied"? Shall we talk about Bosnia? How do you characterize the relationship between the former Soviet Union and what we euphemistically identified as "East Germany"? And insofar as the West Bank is concerned, if the West Bank were intended to be Arab Palestine, why was the region not referred to as "Jordanian-occupied" from 1948 to 1967?

Oxfam Belgium's conduct was both anti-Israel and anti-Jewish, and your explanation that you only meant to boycott occupied territories rests on the slender reed of hypocrisy.

Oxfam Int'l replied:

Oxfam supports the Road Map for peace. We condemn Palestinian suicide bombings and all other acts of terror and violence. We call for the occupation of the Palestinian territories to end. Oxfam is pro-peace and pro-rights, for both Israelis and Palestinians. We have five affiliate groups who are working in the region on long-term development programs and with peace activists on both sides of the conflict.

We want our campaigns to be challenging, but never offensive, and we apologize for any offense that has been caused. Our Belgium affiliate, Oxfam-Solidarité, has amended the campaign page of its website, removed the link to the poster image and introduced a new front-page that gives a more measured explanation of its own involvement in this Belgian campaign. Oxfam in Belgium has also apologized for any offense given.

For the Record

September 10, 2003

To the Editor (Newsday):

Your report (September 10) on the two suicide bombings in Israel yesterday failed to tell the tragedy behind the crimes. Were these murders just tit-for-tat in the Middle East? This incident, when considered with Israel's effort to assassinate Hamas leader Sheikh Yassin, crystallizes the distinction between the Israelis and Palestinians. Yassin survived because Israel intentionally used a small bomb so as to avoid killing innocents in Yassin's proximity. The Palestinians specifically targeted the Café Hillel for the very reason that families and young people were there. Any suggestion of moral equivalency is absurd. *Newsday* should have cried out for the immediate extermination of Hamas and those who do its bidding.

Sadly unmentioned was the fact that two of the Jerusalem victims were Dr. David Applebaum and his 20-year old daughter, Nava. Dr. Applebaum, American born and educated, was head of the emergency room at Shaare Zedek Hospital and founder of the Terem 24-hour emergency clinic in Jerusalem. Ironically, he had just returned from a symposium at NYU where he instructed other physicians how to improve medical services to victims of terrorism. His young daughter, Nava, was to have been married today. Instead, her wedding became her funeral; her "father-in-law" placed her wedding band on her shroud. As a woman buried her husband and her daughter, a young man buried his murdered love.

These heart-breaking facts should have sickened you and rent our hearts and consciences. I weep that they were not even mentioned.

Meanwhile, Hamas's military wing, Izzadin Kassam, welcomed the attack. The group's statement said Israelis could expect more attacks. Crowds in Gaza City celebrated the two attacks by handing out sweets.

November 7, 2003

To the Editor (Newsday):

Israeli Prime Minister Sharon's intention to release hundreds of Palestinian prisoners in exchange for three IDF soldiers, probably dead, and one civilian hostage, again illuminates Israel's continuing moral dilemmas in this conflict. Sharon is entirely correct in refusing to release prisoners "with blood on their hands." Yet I am troubled by the decision to release Hizbullah chief Sheikh Obeid. It is one thing to release the common foot soldier in a war, but the concept of accountability established at Nuremberg requires Israel to keep Obeid under its control. That is, after all, the logic of Israel's policy of decapitating terrorist networks with minimal harm to bystanders.

The release of hundreds of Palestinian prisoners in exchange for four men is, to the outside world perhaps, a lopsided transaction; particularly so where three are presumed dead. Yet it underscores Israel's regard for human life, particularly its men and women in uniform.

Nevertheless, there is one part missing in the equation: IAF Lt. Col. Ron Arad. If a major figure such as Obeid is to be released, why are we not demanding the return of air force navigator Ron Arad or his remains? Perhaps the prime minister is convinced that Hizbullah cannot locate Arad. In that case, we should give them the incentive to do so by refusing to release any prisoners and telling Hizbullah, "Keep looking." Some 400 Palestinians for four or five Jews. The calculus of war is irrelevant to the Palestinians, but not so to the Israelis, and especially not to the family of Ron Arad.

For the Record

December 2, 2003

To the Editor (JP):

It comes as no surprise that former president Carter supports the Geneva initiative. Yet it is to be recalled that Mr. Carter's own foreign policy – and not that of President Bush – is largely responsible for igniting anti-American sentiment around the world. Mr. Carter's foreign policy cost him the White House in 1980 by a landslide vote. Mr. Carter was thrown out of office because the overwhelming majority of the American electorate had no further stomach for his brand of appeasement. Indeed, Mr. Carter never missed an opportunity to confront evil by turning the other cheek. For Mr. Carter to charge that "Bush's inordinate support for Israel...is a source of anti-American sentiment in the world and encourages terror" is audacity and mendacity exponentiated. The assertion that our support for Israel is an acceptable rationale for murder is utterly devoid of moral character.

One might expect Mr. Carter – who claims to be so concerned with the suffering of the Palestinians – to ask how it is that for over 50 years the Palestinian refugees have wallowed in squalor while Arafat and the Palestinian Authority have fattened their own purses to the tune of more than $1 billion?

Although he decries the security fence, Mr. Carter has nothing to say about the fact that it saves lives.

Moreover, Mr. Carter's support for a so-called Palestinian "right of return" – which he surely knows is a formula for the destruction of the Jewish state – corrupts his *bona fides*. It is not enough for Mr. Carter to proclaim his desire for peace. It must be a peace that stops terrorism, saves lives and souls and preserves Israel as a haven for Jews around the world.

Finally, I emphasize that both Mr. Carter and Mr. Beilin and their like-minded Geneva appeasers have failed to win election on these platforms. Frankly, I find Mr. Beilin *et al.* to have participated in treason. Their covert, back door pseudo-policy making smacks of cowardice and monstrous egoism.

December 4, 2003

To the Editor (globe.com):

Tom Wallace's Dec. 3rd Op-Ed piece erroneously attributes malicious intent to Israel in the construction of the security fence. In doing so, Mr. Wallace is inaccurate and misleads his readers. The wall is going up for three reasons: first, Palestinians are killing Israelis; second, no one is doing anything to stop it except the Israelis, and; third, the wall saves lives. Yes, it saves lives. And that is reason enough.

Moreover, Mr. Wallace's assertion that the purpose of the wall is to keep Arabs out of Israel is curious. In fact, there are already close to a million Arabs already living in Israel, many of whom have Israeli citizenship and others who sit in the Knesset. (Can Mr. Wallace identify even one Arab country that allows a Jew to be a citizen, much less a legislator?) But most damning to his assertion is the fact that it is the Palestinians who are demanding – without objection from anyone – that all Israeli settlements must be removed as a precondition to peace. The Palestinians – not the Israelis – would engage in ethnic cleansing of the West Bank.

One final thought: the wall does not prevent Palestinian peace marches…should one ever take place.

For the Record

January 15, 2004

To the Editor (NYT):

Re: "Gaza Mother, 22, Kills Four Israelis in Suicide Bombing" (Jan. 15, 2004). Golda Meir once said there can be no peace between the Arabs and the Israelis until the Arabs love their children more then they hate the Israelis. This 22-year old woman consciously decided that, rather than love and nurture her two children, she would rather "knock on the doors of heaven with the skulls of Zionists." Before the attack, she said, "God will take care of "her children. Her total disregard for life is not nearly as inexplicable as the absence of a maternal instinct. Her legacy to her children is hatred and death. Again, Golda was right.

Israel and the Palestinians – What the Media Aren't Telling You

January 26, 2004

To the Editor (JP):

The statements of Acting Attorney General Edna Arbel are shocking on a number of levels. Politically, her statements that she cannot defend the security fence before the World Court are seditious. She is not a private citizen who has the right to criticize the government's policies. Rather, she is an integral part of the Sharon government and if she cannot support its policies she should resign her post.

Moreover, her statement that Prime Minister Sharon should be indicted is politically unwise and legally unethical. Taken together, her statements cast serious doubt on her ability to do her job without passion or prejudice.

Yet more treacherous than her political sedition are her statements made in the context of being Israel's advocate before the International Court of Justice in The Hague, where international opinion is lining up to build Israel's gallows before the court has even convened.

AG Arbel has forsaken both her role as an advocate and the responsibilities her job entails. She is a lawyer and her client is Israel. If she could not carry its brief, she was obligated to resign her position. Can you imagine any attorney publicly demeaning her client's cause, or stating that her client professes an untenable theory? Ms. Arbel's statements are clear violations of our profession's ethics.

Whatever else she may say about the security fence, it is undisputed that it saves lives. That being the case, and Ms. Arbel opining against it, what does she stand for? As Israel's advocate she is either uninformed or misinformed; perhaps both. But worse yet is her hostility to her client and her abdication of her role to support and defend Israel in a particularly hostile forum. For that alone she must be fired.

For the Record

February 1, 2004

To the Editor (NYT):

Guy Coq's Op-Ed (1/30/04) misses the point. The question in France is not merely how to protect students from religious violence, but rather, why is religious and racial hatred so prevalent? What is it about French society that it serves as a breeding ground for bigotry and what have the French done about it?

The proper response to the beating of Jewish students wearing yarmulkes in Paris was not to tell them not to wear yarmulkes, but for President Chirac to appear on national television and declare that every person in France has the right to peacefully exercise their religion and that the police are to show zero tolerance for hate crimes. Jews should be able to safely wear their yarmulkes, Muslims their scarves, Sikhs their headdress and Christians a crucifix.

The suggestion that France is on the horns of a dilemma is disingenuous. Steps can and must be taken, not only by the government, but also by social leaders, religious institutions and schools. The failure to do so will further entrench France in the cultural fear that has swept across the Middle East and now Western Europe.

Perhaps, if the French had taken such a forceful stand against bigotry when it appeared in the form of anti-Semitism 104 years ago, it would not now be necessary to relearn the meaning of "Liberté, egalité et fraternité."

Israel and the Palestinians – What the Media Aren't Telling You

February 10, 2004

To The Editor (JP):

By constantly harping that the Israeli settlements in Gaza and Judea and Samaria are the source of Palestinian anger, you are missing the point and further encouraging the Palestinians to pluck that string.

The Palestinian-Israeli conflict is not about settlements, or even sovereignty. It is about Israel. The only solution they seek is a "final" solution. How else to explain Arafat's refusals four years ago at Camp David and Taba? As the PLO's security chief implied yesterday, even with total withdrawal from Judea and Samaria and Gaza, no certainty exists that Hamas, Hizbullah and the other terrorists would stop the killing.

The mere existence of a Jewish state gives substance and form to the hatred that has invigorated the Arabs since time immemorial.

Should the settlements be removed, the terrorism would not stop. Should all Jews be removed from the "disputed territories," the Arabs would still seek to destroy the rest of Israel. That is why Arafat walked away from Taba – without the right of return, the Arabs can only secure all of Israel through murder.

So it is. So has it always been.

For the Record

March 23, 2004

To the Editor (JP):

It came as no surprise to learn that Shimon Peres was against the targeted killing of Hamas leader Sheikh Ahmed Yassin. Peres long ago established his credentials as an appeaser at Oslo and Madrid. His political philosophy of wishful thinking has survived the Passover massacre in Netanya, the suicide bombing that murdered kids at the Dolphinarium, the capture of the *Karine-A*, and so much more. What is remarkable is the ease with which he has endured the suffering of others.

Indeed, he has turned the other cheek so often his knee-jerk propitiation of aggression pales in comparison to that of the late British prime minister Neville Chamberlain.

Although the record strongly suggests that Mr. Peres is not a pacifist, his ability to ignore the bald-faced lying of Arafat and the cold-blooded murder of so many innocents is indicative of a mind incapable of distilling reality from treachery. His obsessive need to resolve this conflict at the negotiating table while Hamas murders scores of Israelis under his very nose bespeaks a moral constitution utterly devoid of mettle and nerve. Worse than an appeaser, he is a coward.

Israel and the Palestinians – What the Media Aren't Telling You

March 23, 2004

To the Editor (NYT):

Your front page headline identifying Hamas founder and leader Sheikh Yassin as a "cleric" was an insult to every man, woman and child murdered or maimed by Hamas. Such a characterization suggests a man of peace rather than the dissembler and merchant of hate that he was. I don't suppose your headlines in 1945 said "Allies Take Berlin, Austrian Painter Believed Dead"? The gray lady is too old to be cute and too smart to be disingenuous.

For the Record

March 23, 2004

To the Editor (Newsday):

Your prediction about the cycle of violence certain to follow the killing of Hamas founder and leader Sheikh Yassin is undeniable. The problem lies in the assignment of blame. I suggest that Israel had every right – indeed, the obligation to its citizens – to kill Yassin. To argue that Israel was wrong requires the conclusion that Israel should not either have or exercise its right of self-defense.

What would you have Prime Minister Sharon do when scores of Israelis are murdered at a Passover table in Netanya, having coffee in Haifa, traveling to school in public buses or socializing at a club in Tel Aviv? Negotiate with Hamas? What's there to negotiate? Sit back and do nothing? More death. Rely on the Palestinian Authority to rein in the terrorists? The PA has already said it won't do that. Wait for the UN to step in? Not likely since Kofi Annan, you will recall, stated at the notorious Durban Conference that the Jews should stop harping on the Holocaust for sympathy. This is urban guerrilla warfare in which the Palestinians build bomb factories next to schools and use children and young mothers to commit suicide-bombings. Thus, Israel must protect her citizens with all the power at her disposal from those who would murder them with all the power at their disposal.

In a hostile and hateful world – where the Palestinians have no respect for life and lack even the basic maternal instinct found near the bottom of the taxonomic chart – Israel has to take the issue of self-defense into her own hands, and to condemn her for doing so is indefensible and contrary to international as well as natural law.

As for ascribing blame, I recall the story of the school bully who came home with a bloody nose and torn clothes. When his mother asked him what happened, he said, "It all started when the other kid hit me back."

Israel and the Palestinians – What the Media Aren't Telling You

April 1, 2004

To the Editor (JP)

Re: Temple Mount Faithful Barred. The jurisprudence of civil conflict has always held that when two adverse parties wish to visit the same site it is the obligation of the law to remove the one who threatens or violates the rights of the other to peacefully assemble. To act otherwise – regardless of motive – is to reward intolerance and punish the peaceful exercise of one's rights. You cannot keep the peace at the expense of denying people a fundamental freedom (in this case, the right to practice one's religion peacefully) in order to avoid a violent confrontation with those who are intolerant and violent. To do so transposes rights and wrongs, and caters to violence. Conduct contrary to the concept of freedom is rewarded while those who respect the rights of others are punished. Violence trumps tolerance and intolerance vetoes peace. The ban on Jews and Christians from visiting the Temple Mount has been such a form of appeasement.

It is unfortunate that the High Court of Justice has denied an ultra-nationalist Jewish group access to the Temple Mount. By doing so, the court has rewarded Palestinian violence against Jews who seek to visit or pray there. This is particularly troubling in light of the fact that there is no evidence that the Jews had any violent intent.

In a multicultural democracy – into which category alas Israel falls – the rights of all people to peaceably assemble and pray is fundamental. The High Court should not have validated the Palestinian desire to make the Temple Mount *Judenrein*. Of course, these threats are consistent with the Palestinian laws denying Jews access to our holy sites under Palestinian jurisdiction, and I expect no better from people who would destroy a holy Jewish site and rebuild a mosque in its place. As Jews we hold ourselves to higher standards of morality.

What the High Court should have done was to permit a peaceful assembly at the Temple Mount by anyone and to provide police protection against those who would assault them. Instead, we have the image of the High Court and the rule of law being kidnapped by the threat of violence against Jews who would peacefully visit the Temple Mount, a site, by the way, holy to more people than just the Palestinians. What does this portend for the future?

In a democracy, it is the government's duty to protect the rights of its citizens in the peaceful exercise of their various religions. Sometimes that may require police action, but only against those who would deny that right to others. The closing of the Temple Mount to Jews and Christians was such an event.

Israel and the Palestinians – What the Media Aren't Telling You

April 16, 2004

To the Editor (Newsday):

The outrage expressed by the Arabs, Europeans and even some of the American media over President Bush's comment that the United States does not favor a Palestinian "right" of return comes as little surprise. It also comes with the familiar histrionics: name-calling ("racist," "apartheid," etc.); Palestinian threats (more suicide bombers, relentless violence, etc.); and the usual UN and EU condemnations. They are all familiar. They are all fairly typical. Your editorial ("Settlements Over Peace," April 15, 2004) contains a flawed position about the Arab-Israeli conflict; i.e., that the so-called "right of return" is an important negotiating point for the Israelis and Palestinians to work out between themselves.

Yet to argue that this aspect of the Arab-Israeli conflict is a crucial point for negotiations misses the mark on two counts: First, the Palestinians have utterly failed, and are seemingly incapable of, providing Israel with a bona fide peace partner. Inasmuch as the overwhelming majority of Palestinians favor continued terrorism, Abbas and Qurei are merely doing their bidding. Second, and most important, is that Israel can never agree to any form of "right of return."

For 56 years, the Arabs have offered Israel only death by war and terrorism. By arguing that the "right of return" is open to negotiation, Israel is given the alternative of suicide. The demographics are indisputable. To allow the Palestinians to return would eventually leave an Israeli democracy at the whim of an Arab majority. Not since the Babylonians of the 6th century BCE have Arabs been tolerant of a Jewish minority. Israel will never negotiate its very essence, its raison d'être, indeed, its existence. To think otherwise is foolhardy, presumptuous and self-indulgent.

Thus, the "right of return" is as hemlock to Israel. It is a proposition which should never be open for negotiation and it is long past the time to say so. And that is all President Bush has done: clear away some of the smoke. The democratic and Jewish nature of Israel is written in stone. It is immutable. That the Palestinians will not accept that fundamental truth is strong evidence that the issue is not the West Bank or Gaza. The issue is Israel herself.

Israel and the Palestinians – What the Media Aren't Telling You

Around April 23, 2004, "The Medium," the student newspaper at Rutgers University published a front-page cartoon takeoff of the old carnival game "hit-the-target-and-dunk-the-clown." Only this time, it wasn't a clown, but a Jew, and it wasn't into a vat of water he was sent.

April 23, 2004

To the Editor:

I learned just today about the so-called "cartoon" on the cover of *The Medium*. There is little to be gained by responding directly to *The Medium*'s staff or faculty adviser. What I have to say is for the rest of the Rutgers family.

Although the First Amendment may well protect *The Medium*'s cartoon, the concept of academic freedom does not. Not every crackpot has the right to say whatever he or she wants, wherever they want. It is one thing to protect the right of these people to express their views (however horrific), and it is quite another to insist that they have the right to do so with the imprimatur of the university's support. Rutgers' good name, funds, faculty and facilities are being used to promote *The Medium*. They operate out of university property, the Student Activities Center, and they have a faculty adviser.

Just as a person has the right to his opinions, he doesn't have the right to say them in my home. Rutgers should take the position that *The Medium* may print and distribute hateful opinions, but it may not do so with the university's cooperation or funds or on university property. Throw them out of the Student Activities Center. If *The Medium* advocated apartheid, I have no doubt the Rutgers community would rise up as one and toss the miscreants to the street.

In the meantime, there is an appropriate response, which is both legal and ethical: Treat those responsible for this disgrace the same way we would treat a leper: isolation/quarantine. You must shun the people on its staff who were a part of this exercise in prejudice. Do not greet them; do not speak to them. When they walk by, turn your backs to them. If they sit down at your table, get up and move. Refuse to be in their company. Refuse to have anything to so do with them.

The entire university community – not just the Jewish students and faculty – must make it clear that uncivilized behavior is anathema to all. I doubt that quarantine will change their minds, but the entire university must take a stand. This is not just a matter of taste or etiquette. This is about character.

The New York Times reported that several dozen former British diplomats presented a letter to Prime Minister Blair condemning the government's Middle East policy.

April 27, 2004

To the Editor (NYT):

How disingenuous it is of these British ex-diplomats to criticize Prime Minister Blair for "abandoning important principles of neutrality in the Holy Land." Did the British expect, or receive, American neutrality prior to America's entry into World War II? Was Lend-Lease an act of neutrality? The existence of a dispute does not require neutrality. This particularly so in matters of war and peace, where it is often clear who has been the provocateur. There is no moral equivalence between Israeli democracy and the Palestinian culture of hatred.

As reported earlier, the British already have their hands full with militant Islam. Shall they retain the balance of neutrality after the first suicide bomber strikes in Piccadilly or the Underground? Have these gentlemen learned nothing from Munich?

On May 2, 2004, a young Israeli woman and her four daughters were in Gaza driving back to their home in Gush Katif when two Palestinians shot up the car and murdered them all: Tali Hatuel, a 34-year-old social worker, then eight months pregnant, and her four daughters Hila, 11, Hadar, 9, Roni, 7, and Merav, 2. The May 3, 2004 report of National Public Radio's Julie McCarthy implied that the fault lay with the Hatuels, because the presence of settlers in Gaza had provoked bloodshed. This letter was sent to the president and CEO of NPR in Washington, DC.

May 3, 2004

Dear Mr. Klose:

This morning your Julie McCarthy reported on the murder of a pregnant Israeli woman and her four children. First the car was shot at by two terrorists to bring it to a stop. Advancing to the car, the murderers shot the pregnant mother to death in front of her four daughters, and then murdered the three girls in the back seat. To emphasize their point, one of the murderers walked to the passenger side of the car where the two-year-old infant girl Merav was still strapped into her car seat. He fired three shots point blank into her head. The Palestinians are believed to have videotaped the massacre. Afterwards, Palestinian leader Yassir Arafat called the dead Hatuels "terrorists" and proclaimed the two murderers "heroic martyrs."

Why did this happen? What had these four young girls and their pregnant mother done to bring such slaughter to themselves? Your reporter provided a remarkable answer: "There was ample evidence yesterday to show that their [Israeli settlers] continued presence in Gaza is provoking bloodshed." Thus, the Jewish victims, solely by virtue of their presence, brought this despicable fate upon themselves. Did your reporter even identify the murderers as "terrorists?" No. They were "Palestinian gunmen." Nor did she recall that Arafat himself called the killers "heroic martyrs" and the dead girls "terrorists." Why?

That this report was biased and unethical is all too obvious.

But more than that, it bespoke favoritism and its illegitimate stepchild – prejudice. Ms. McCarthy pandered to the hateful mob here, the Palestinians, and proposed to excuse this unspeakable atrocity against a pregnant woman and her daughters.

In this war, which the Palestinians have chosen to make "to the death," we have a choice to support either a democratic Israel fighting for her life or a Palestinian culture of death and hatred. That NPR should have chosen the latter is explicable only in terms of anti-Semitism.

Imagine the outpouring of anger at Israel had her soldiers done the same thing to a Palestinian family. NPR holds Israelis and Palestinians to two very different standards and that is why it is anti-Semitic. It seems NPR has given your reporter a "get out of jail free" card. NPR disclaimers abound – all lacking credibility and sincerity.

These are serious charges and should be of concern to NPR, which sups, after all, at the public trough. But regardless of what you or NPR do or say, today, a young man buried his pregnant wife and their four girls. I cannot imagine the depth of his inconsolable grief and despair.

For the Record

May 7, 2004

To the Editor:

Re: Nazi Slogans Scrawled on French Jews' Memorial. "Shocked! I am shocked to learn that gambling is going on in this establishment!" said Claude Rains as he was handed his share of the evening's profits in the movie *Casablanca*.

Recently another spate of anti-Semitic vandalism at Jewish cemeteries and assaults on yeshiva students in Paris has caused the French, under the leadership of Jacques Chirac, to ban the wearing of religious items in public. Not just *kippot*, but conspicuously Islamic clothing has been banned from the streets of the City of Light.

How did this happen? Anti-Semitism has a long and distinguished history in *toute la France*. But, to see how this current generation of Jew-haters came to be does not require us to go back as far as the Dreyfus case, or even to the Vichy government. Current examples abound. Culturally and politically, Jean-Marie Le Pen has been inciting Jew-hatred for years. Instead of quarantining him like the pariah he should be, Le Pen and his political allies have found a niche for themselves in the political and social landscape. Rather than diminishing, his influence has thrived. Rather than being shunned by the "intelligentsia," he is the darling of Paris parlor parties. Out of his mouth we'll hear no denunciations of those who do not let even the dead rest in peace.

Then there is *Monsieur le Président* Chirac. Here we need go back no further than his recent trip to Israel when Netanyahu was prime minister. Chirac's arrogance was conspicuous, particularly when the cameras were rolling. He constantly complained about his treatment – Netanyahu made sure Chirac had bodyguards around him at all times. He seemed to go out of his way to sympathize with the Palestinians and rebuke the Israelis, who were clearly annoying to him.

What sort of response did he expect from his countrymen? The Jews had harassed their president and were torturing the poor Palestinians. There have been many incidents of public anti-Semitism in the past few years. And what do the French do? They myopically pass this foolish law outlawing the public wearing of religious garb and symbols. Punish the victim.

Chirac should have ordered all law enforcement agencies to hunt down the miscreants and put them in jail. Why was a presidential directive not read in every school in France and from the pulpit of every religious institution stating unequivocally that prejudice is hateful to all of France and its soul? So far as I know, not one person has been arrested for the desecration of Jewish cemeteries or for assaulting students identifiable as Jewish by dint of their clothes.

Finally, with the second desecration in about a month, Chirac made a public statement denouncing vandalism of the Jewish cemeteries, declaring it unbecoming of the citizens of France. He is shocked! Shocked! he says, to see Jew-hatred in France!

Apparently, not all Frenchmen are equal. Shocking.

For the Record

June 17, 2004

To the Editor (JP):

The incidents of violence and intimidation against British contractors at a project to build 435 modern apartments for the residents of the Jenin refugee camp come as no surprise. Indeed, it is thoroughly consistent with the past conduct of the Palestinians and their leaders.

Why would people living in the squalor of a refugee camp act against what is obviously in their best interests? We learn one reason from one of the refugees: possible loss of refugee status. It is well beyond comprehension why any person would treasure refugee status, except with an ulterior motive. It is apparently worth the loss of one's dignity to be viewed as oppressed and a victim. That they should choose such a role for themselves, however, is not nearly so baffling as why they would intentionally do this to their children.

Another answer lies in the political philosophy of the Palestinian leadership. It is in the interest of the PA to keep its people homeless, hungry, angry and unemployed. That is what seeds fertile ground for Hamas, hatred and suicide bombers. Without that hatred – and someone against whom to direct it – it would not be quite so easy to recruit children to strap explosives onto their young bodies.

Moreover, preservation of the refugee camps advances the PA's public relations war against Israel. The Western media need no excuse to chastise Israel. Words about who is doing what to whom doesn't harm Israel's public image nearly as well as photographs and film of children playing in dust and squalor.

Finally, what would the Palestinians – refugees or not – do if they found out that the Palestinian Authority had received hundreds of millions of dollars that could have been used to tear down all the refugee camps and replace them with decent housing? Who do you suppose benefits from that ignorance? Is it not remarkable the fortitude with which the PA bears the suffering of its citizens? All of this reminds us that the Israeli-Palestinian conflict is not about helping the Palestinians.

Israel and the Palestinians – What the Media Aren't Telling You

30 July 2004

To the Editor (JP):

Sir,

I find it necessary to respond to your letter of 24 July past in the *Jerusalem Post*. You set the tone of your letter by telling Israel that the EU and the ICJ are going to ride herd on Israel whether she likes it or not. Frankly, that's little more than a condescending poke in the eye. You seek to justify this presumptuousness under the banner of international law, which is sheer nonsense. Anyone who knows anything about realpolitik and international law is certain of one thing, if nothing else: international law is what the most influential party says it is. In the United Nations, the European Union and the International Court of Justice, notions of morality or jurisprudential right and wrong are irrelevant. For 30 years, the UN, Europeans and ICJ have shown themselves to be consummately anti-Israel. There is not enough space here to itemize the bill of indictment, but I note the ICJ's vote on the security fence and the EU member countries' vote in the General Assembly as sufficient for the time being.

The court's opinion was a mere tautology: First, every country has the right to protect its citizens against foreign aggression. Second, the Palestinian terrorists are not part of a recognized country's militia. Ergo, the right does not exist. You and so many others just don't get it. The fence is not about land. It is not about the Green Line. It is not about restrictions on Palestinian travel. It is not about Palestinians earning a living. The fence is about saving lives: Israeli lives (both Arab and Jewish). Because killers entered Israel so easily and casually to murder women and children, Israel had to put a stop to it. No one else would.

There is not a single UN or EU resolution condemning suicide bombers, much less the use of women and children suicide bombers, to kill Israelis. Why do you suppose that is? Did international law intervene when some 20 kids were murdered at a Tel Aviv discotheque? Which EU proponent of international law spoke up when murder was committed at the Sbarro pizzeria in Jerusalem? Can you name a single EU leader who spoke out when a café in Jerusalem was bombed, killing an emergency room doctor who distinguished himself by saving the lives of victims of terrorist attacks, and his daughter who was to be married the next day?

Do you see the pattern? Palestinian kills Israelis and nobody cares, much less decries the killings. There are no resolutions in the General Assembly. There are no pronouncements out of the EU. Germany, France, Italy, Denmark and Great Britain are suddenly struck mute.

You decry the hardships of the Palestinians, yet the Palestinians suffer because Arafat wants and needs to point to Israel as the source of their misery.

How did Arafat personally acquire about $1 billion in foreign accounts? Do you think he made wise investments in the stock market? Did he give up smoking or join the global effort to recycle aluminum cans for a nickel? Do you think he stole money from the church plate? Why is it that the squalid, stinking refugee camps have not been destroyed and replaced with livable housing?

The answers are the same: it suits Arafat's long term goal of destroying Israel from Tel Aviv to Jerusalem and from Safed to Eilat. Hundreds of millions of dollars have been gifted to the Palestinian Authority, but what have they done with it to better the lives of their people? Nothing. Can you begin to imagine how many new homes and hospitals could have been built with all that money? And do you know how many actually have been built? None. In fact, about six weeks ago, a foreign construction company that was going to build new housing for the Palestinians picked up and left. Why? They and their families had been threatened by the Palestinians.

You do admit "that the fence has saved many lives," but opine that "it would also have saved these lives had it been built inside [the pre-1967 armistice line]." In fact, there have been terrorist attempts even where the fence was inside the Green Line.

Specifically, two months ago two young Palestinians planned to go into an Israeli town in the West Bank and attack a school. (That's right, a school.) The killings were prevented because the would-be murderers found that they had to travel around many kilometers of fence, and in that extra time, the IDF was able to track them down and arrest them. The security fence is a non-violent and reasonable response to murder. Many lives have been saved by the fence. Not one life has been lost by it.

So, you told us "from square one that we oppose the construction of the wall in occupied Palestinian territory"? This is not the time or place to debate the so-called occupation, but it is appropriate to point out that Israeli troops have only gone where the lives of Israelis have been taken or threatened. Israel merely seeks to physically isolate the killers and keep them out of her neighborhood.

Finally, I ask you whether any other country in the world would be excoriated for protecting its citizens. How did the UN respond when Germany destroyed – as well it should have – the Baader-Meinhof Gang? or when Japan rooted out the Red Army? or when Great Britain fought IRA terrorism? or when Italy killed off the Red Brigades? Did the UN or a single European country have the temerity to tell even one of those nations not to protect its citizens? Your collective hypocrisy smells worse than those refugee camps.

You claim that the EU is in the peace process whether Israel likes it or not? Don't count on it. We know you for what you are and what you stand for. And you will never dictate to Israel the terms under which you will let her live…or make her die.

For the Record

August 6, 2004

To the Editor:

It came as no surprise that three Palestinians were murdered in cold blood, in a hospital no less, by other Palestinians, because it was thought that the three were spying for Israel. One of the three dead men was in intensive care, the three having just been injured by a PA policeman who threw a grenade into their jail cell in Gaza. So much for the rule of law.

I mention this only to underline the hypocrisy of most of the Europeans when dealing with Israel and the Palestinians. The International Court of Justice dragged Israel over the coals for trying to protect her citizens (Arab and Jew) from terrorists hell-bent on murder. The Palestinian Authority killed three men thought to be "collaborators" working with the Israelis, and the European/UN reaction is a chilling silence. What happened to the rule of law they so warmly embraced? Did the victims receive the slightest scintilla of due process? (Of course not, since in Gaza due process comes out of the barrel of an AK-47.) Did the brave French demand that arrests be made? Did the sedate Germans call for a commission of inquiry? Not even our jurisprudential cousins, the British, asked whether there was any evidence. The Tanzim benignly replied that they don't need evidence.

Israel responded to murder with a non-violent fence. Even this much was tacitly accepted by the ICJ: No lives are lost and many are saved. Yet, with the exception of 10 votes against, and a handful of abstentions, the General Assembly voted overwhelmingly to condemn the fence and demanded that Israel pay reparations.

All this while human rights and the rule of law find no succor or solace in the land that would be Palestine. An ancient Greek tragedy being played out in the 21st century? You bet it is.

August 9, 2004

To the Editor (JP):

Mr. Muessigbrod's letter (August 8, 2004) chastises Israeli and Diaspora Jews for charging the EU and the UN with anti-Semitism because of their vote condemning Israel's security fence. We're all crying wolf, he says, and eventually the charge will lose its meaning. We do not make charges of anti-Semitism lightly, but rather to remind you of who you are and what you are doing.

Mr. Muessigbrod has it all wrong. Israel has taken its fair share of criticism over the years without having posited that explanation. Nevertheless, where anti-Semitism is present, it is appropriate to call it what it is.

Muessigrob asks if the "UN, ICJ, the EU...we Germans (of course), the French, the Spaniards are anti-Semitic, and the BBC are anti-Semitic." He then sarcastically asks, "Perhaps the bad weather and the road accidents are signs of anti-Semitism, too." The point he tries to make is neither apposite nor clever. In this instance, at least, yes, all those nations and institutions have shown anti-Semitism. Why? Because they hold Israel to a standard to which they hold no other countries; because they deny Israel, and no other country, the right to protect its citizens; because the ICJ was comprised of several judges whose own personal anti-Semitism had been well documented before the case was even presented, making them unfit to serve on the panel.

A recent poll found that 75% of EU citizens believe Israel to be the greatest threat to world peace. Unlike the British, French and Germans, Israel has never initiated an offensive military campaign. Unlike Iran, Syria and Saudi Arabia, Israel does not export terrorism around the world. Unlike the now democratic Russians and the benign French, Israel does not contribute to nuclear proliferation among dictators. And, unlike every Arab state, Israel has no law that discriminates on the basis of religion in citizenship, voting, holding elective office or even owning property.

Israelis are being murdered in the street, on buses, in

schools, cafes, discotheques and pizzerias. Those are acts of real anti-Semitism and for Muessigrob to say that the accusation of anti-Semitism is used for "lack of better arguments" is insulting to us and demeaning to himself. For all those nations and organizations to condemn the Jewish state for a peaceful act of self-defense was indeed an act of overt anti-Semitism or cowardly appeasement of the Arabs. Probably both.

August 16, 2004

To the Editor (JP):

Re: "Beacon of Light." The sentiments in Doris Cadigan's letter, stating that "God's purpose for Israel to be a beacon of light," was in terms of offering justice and mercy – not military might. Had Israel not had a superior military, several things are certain: First, we would be saying *kaddish* for the members of the Haganah and a stillborn Israel. Second, the Six Day War would have had an entirely different meaning. Third, the Yom Kippur War would have marked the destruction of the Third Commonwealth. Fourth, Palestinians would be playing handball against the Western Wall and again using Jewish graves on the Mount of Olives as toilets. Fifth, Jewish holy sites would be torn down as was the case in Shechem (Nablus). And finally, the Iraqi nuclear site at Osirak would have become operational, the consequences of which I hope I don't have to spell out.

The only thing that prevented these catastrophes was the strength of the IDF. And because of that, men, women and children may pray at the Western Wall, visit the Mount of Olives, study at the Hebrew University, read the Dead Sea Scrolls and practice Judaism freely. And Christians, Muslims and all others may peacefully practice their religions anywhere in Israel.

For the Record

August 24, 2004

To the Editor (JP):

As the EU and the UN struggle to force Yassir Arafat on the Israelis, it is appropriate to ask whether there truly can be peace between the Israelis and the Palestinians? How has each society acted to bring understanding to the other? How have they treated each other?

The example of six-year old Palestinian Mahdi Abu Snaibeh, reported last week, is a revealing lesson in both the Palestinian psyche and values. Young Mahdi was severely injured – and his grandfather killed – when another Palestinian remotely set off a bomb at an Israeli checkpoint last week. The Palestinian hospital couldn't save Mahdi, so he was evacuated to the pediatric care unit at Hadassah Hospital in Jerusalem. Asked to comment, Mahdi's father said "this is our destiny" and went on to blame the Israelis for his lot in life even as Israeli doctors working only meters away saved his son's life.

Consider in contrast, the execution-style murder of pregnant Tali Hatuel and her four daughters two months ago.

Palestinians murder with the approval of the Palestinian Authority and kill Israel's young even as Israelis struggle to save the lives of Palestinian youths.

Israel and the Palestinians – What the Media Aren't Telling You

August 26, 2004

To the Editor:

Aaron Bergman's approach to resolving the Arab-Israeli conflict ("wait patiently") is simplistic and his suggestion that Arafat's removal from the *dramatis personae* is "crucial to...peace and reconciliation," while desirable, is unlikely to have a causal effect on the conflict. Consider these statistics from a recent Palestinian poll: More than 70% of Palestinians favor continuing the war against Israel even if they receive an independent state including all of the West Bank, Gaza, and East Jerusalem; 80% of Palestinians refuse to relinquish the so-called "right of return," which is a demographic euphemism for destruction of the Jewish state; 75% of Palestinians support the suicide bombers murdering Israeli civilians; and, 63% of Palestinians believe the 9/11 hijackers were not terrorists.

The Israeli-Palestinian conflict is not over who controls the West Bank, Gaza or Jerusalem. And its end will not come about through patience. Its end will come about only upon the end of hatred. Consider the covenant of the terrorist group Hamas: after Israel is destroyed, the only Jews who will be permitted to remain are those who will have converted to Islam.

Patience suggests that a cooling of passions will diffuse antipathy and conflict. But how much time is necessary? Since the Russian pogroms? The Dreyfus affair? The Holocaust? The Hebron massacres in the 1920s and '30s? Since the Yom Kippur War?

Since the 1974 murder of 27 Israelis – 21 of them children – at the schoolhouse in Ma'alot? Muslim extremists have hijacked the Koran and call daily for Muslims to kill every Jew on sight, while at the Durban conference, Nobel Peace laureate Kofi Annan accused Jews of harping on the Holocaust to evoke sympathy.

Too recent? Need more time to heal? Is 350 years, since 1648–49, when the Cossacks of Chmielnicki massacred tens of thousands of us? How about 515 years from 1492 when the Inquisition reigned and Spain expelled all Jews who would not convert to Christianity? Since the Crusades, almost a millennium ago? Since the 1st century CE when the Romans murdered over 30% of the Jews of Judea and Samaria and destroyed the great Temple of Solomon? Since the Common Era began some 2,000 years ago, while churches of all denominations accused us of deicide?

Israel doesn't need patience. She needs an end to anti-Semitism. And I can think of six million reasons why Israel must protect its citizens, not with patience, but with every means at her disposal.

Israel and the Palestinians – What the Media Aren't Telling You

September 2, 2004

Mr. Sullivan,

Let me respond to your letter. The decision of the International Court of Justice was not made solely on the basis of boundaries. Bear in mind that the Palestinians urged removal of the entire fence, not just where it allegedly encroaches on so-called Palestinian territory – a point adopted by the ICJ.

Insofar as boundaries are concerned, I find it disingenuous of the PA to argue about boundaries when it refuses to negotiate with Israel on that, or any other, subject. For the sake of argument, let's assume that the issue of boundaries is seminal. The Palestinians themselves want borders, but they won't negotiate with Israel on the subject. Too clever by half. They fight for boundaries, yet they won't negotiate for them and, therefore, think they have the right to kill Israelis because they don't have what they won't negotiate for. Israel, placed in a Catch-22 situation, is upbraided for simply trying to save its citizens' lives.

Inasmuch as the Palestinian Authority won't negotiate for boundaries – and uses that self-created excuse to commit murder – Israel has no alternative but to create her own boundaries. If the Palestinians don't like Sharon's boundaries, let them sit down at a table and show him what they do want. Of course, that won't happen because the PA wants all of Israel. And dare I remind you that Israel offered the Palestinians 96 % of Judea and Samaria, all of Gaza, and Jerusalem as a shared capital. Arafat's response was the current state of war. So much for the argument over boundaries.

Finally, the fence is about one thing: security. Where the security fence exists, suicide bombings have decreased dramatically. Where it does not exist, the bombings continue. The massacre in Be'er Sheva bears testament to that. In plain English, the fence is about murder.

Mr. Sullivan, Israel has been told not to build a security fence that is necessary to protect its civilian population from Palestinian murder. All other arguments about the fence are irrelevant. Israel is told she cannot exercise her right of self-defense. No other country in history has been given such a despicable command. Only Israel.

Israel and the Palestinians – What the Media Aren't Telling You

September 2, 2004

To the Editor (NYT):

It was heart-rending to see photos of the Be'er Sheva bus with a dead child hanging out of a window. I can only begin to imagine the despair of that child's parents.

But we saw only half the equation. How much more enlightening it would have been had there also been a photo alongside showing the Palestinians of Gaza firing their rifles in the air, handing out candy and celebrating in the streets the murder of Israeli children. Why did you not report that side of the story?

What follows is a response to a letter published in The Jerusalem Post from a doctor in Nablus.

September 3, 2004

Dear Doctor,

You blame the Israelis because you do not have a country. How many times has Israel offered you a Palestinian nation and every time your dictator Arafat has said "No!" In 2000, Barak and President Clinton offered your people a new nation on 96% of Judea and Samaria, all of Gaza and half of Jerusalem. Much less than take that generous offer, even less than offering a counter-proposal, Arafat walked away, returned to Ramallah and set off the second intifada, which we learn was his plan before he even went to Camp David regardless of what transpired there. In other words, there was going to be an intifada regardless of what Israel offered the Palestinians. Your response to the olive branch has been bullets and bombs loaded with ball bearings to maximize pain, injury and death.

You don't like the security fence and are humiliated by check-points? Then stop sending suicide-bombers who do in fact target civilians.

Rather than address every point in your letter, let me make the following observation. The Israelis want peace. There are dozens of groups demonstrating in public for an end to what you call the "occupation." There are peace marches all over Israel. Peace demonstrations of tens of thousands of people in Israel's cities. Yet I know of no instance of a peace march by the Palestinians. Not one.

There is no Palestinian peace movement anywhere. Not in Gaza. Not in Nablus. Not in Jericho. Not in Bethlehem. Why is that? The only conclusion I can draw is that the Palestinians do not want peace with Israel. They only want peace without Israel. It isn't going to happen that way. Never. You teach your children to hate and to be martyrs for the glory of killing Jews. You send your young mothers and children out with dynamite strapped to their chests and say, "Go kill Jews." I ask you to stop the killings for the sake of your own sons and daughters. Their lives will be your legacy.

It is not up to Arafat to make peace. It is up to you Palestinians, all of you; mothers, fathers, doctors, laborers, merchants, schoolteachers and stonemasons. *You* decide your fate. In the last 15 years, dictators have been run out of Haiti, the Philippines and every country in Eastern Europe. The mighty Soviet Union has crumbled. Are the Palestinians incapable of wresting their lives and future from the Palestinian Authority? Your future is in your own hands.

For the Record

September 7, 2004

To the Editor (JP):

After the IDF killed 14 Hamas terrorists in response to the double suicide-murders in Be'er Sheva, the Palestinian prime minister states that "any" retaliation by Hamas would be justified. Then, Hamas spokesperson Mushir al-Masri vowed to continue the firing of Kassam rockets, even specifically at Israeli children. Thus do the PA and Hamas attempt to create a moral equivalence between murderers and schoolchildren.

The intentional targeting of children by Palestinian terrorists is uniquely cruel, wicked and heartless. Israel has exercised restraint as the Palestinians have murdered people at work, in cafes and restaurants, teenagers in discotheques, people in buses, etc. Even a member of her cabinet and a two-year-old infant in her car seat. Now we are told that children will be specific targets.

The actions which Hamas and the PA seek to justify are so far beyond any accepted norm of warfare that they must be met with a rejoinder so strong as to command consent by what little is left of civilization. The targeted killing of children is so vast and horrific a violation of international law that the Palestinians must know that to do so will carry immediate and enormous consequences.

September 24, 2004

Dear Mr. Jukes (Reuters):

It appears that Reuters has a problem with the English language. This is surprising coming from the land of Chaucer, Shakespeare, Pope and Churchill. As I understand it, Reuters refuses to identify Arab murderers as terrorists. (You will agree, won't you, that they are murderers?)

I wonder if you are consistent in your international reporting. Did Reuters refer to the IRA as freedom fighters when Lord Mountbatten was murdered? Two weeks ago, did you run a story about Chechan "freedom fighters" in Beslan? And how would you describe the Palestinian who murdered two-year-old Merav Hatuel while still strapped into her car seat? Whose lives and freedom were advanced by those murders?

You refer to Gaza, Judea and Samaria as "occupied." Why is it that Reuters has never referred to "Syrian occupied" Lebanon, or "Russian occupied" Chechnya. Between 1945 and 1990, did you ever refer to "Soviet occupied" Poland, Czechoslovakia, Hungary, or Germany? Do you see a pattern?

Do you see Reuters as fulfilling its principal function of reporting the news without bias and prejudice? Perhaps you will feel differently when al-Qaida suicide-bombers detonate a bomb in the Piccadilly Underground at rush hour.

Adlai Stevenson once said that credibility is to a newspaper what virtue is to a lady. Reuters, however, needs to restore both its credibility and its virtue.

For the Record

September 28, 2004

To the Editor (IHT):

Jonathan Power's article of 22 September about Israel, Iran and nuclear power, which states that Iran has more to fear from Israel than Israel does from Iran, seems to confuse the vulture with its prey. Not once since Israel allegedly acquired nuclear technology has it threatened any nation with the use of that weapon. Unlike its Arab neighbors, Israel has never used chemical or biological weapons against any nation or people.

Iran's leaders, on the other hand, have seemingly gone out of their way to make it clear that their *raison d'être* is the destruction of Israel, which they refer to as "the Zionist enemy." Destroy Israel and kill all its Jews, they urge. Iran's leaders have variously stated: "The foundation of the Islamic regime is opposition to Israel, and the perpetual object of Iran is the elimination of Israel from the region"; "The cancerous tumor called Israel must be uprooted from the region." Former president Rafsanjani called the establishment of Israel "the worst event in history," declared his intention to decimate Israel, clarifying that "one [nuclear] bomb is enough to destroy all Israel," and threatening that "in due time, the Islamic world will have a military nuclear device."

Mr. Power's point of view flies in the face of history and suggests an invidious motive.

The Presbyterian Church announced a plan to divest itself of companies which do business with Israel. In response to criticism, the Church decried the "horrors of a military occupation...of Palestinian lands" by the Israelis.

Israel and the Palestinians – What the Media Aren't Telling You

October 1, 2004

Mr. John Detterick,

I have reviewed your general reply to the questions over the Presbyterian Church's proposed divestment plan arising out of what you call Israel's occupation of so-called Palestinian land. I feel that a response is appropriate, but first I have some questions:

1. Other than South Africa, has the PC ever divested itself of companies doing business in any other country? Spain under Franco? The Soviet Union under Stalin? Under Khrushchev? Under Brezhnev? Uganda under Idi Amin? Romania under Ceausescu? Perhaps Iraq under Saddam Hussein? What about China after Tiananmen Square?

2. Who started the violence? And against whom was it directed? Wasn't the "occupation" of the West Bank and Gaza the result of Israel's June 1967 war of self-defense and to root out terrorists, thereby protecting Israel's citizens, both Jewish and Arab?

3. Arab Israelis sit in the Knesset. How many Jews sit in the parliament of any Arab country? Israel has outlawed political parties such as Kach that urge the expulsion of all Arabs from Israel. Why must the West Bank and Gaza become *Judenrein*? Does the PC support the Palestinians on this point? And if so, do you agree with the other side of the coin that all Arabs should be expelled from Israel?

4. When did the West Bank and Gaza become occupied? If these territories became "occupied territories" in 1967 when Israel won the Six Day War, why weren't they Jordanian-occupied territories from 1949 to 1967? Between 1949 and 1967, did the PC engage in divestment from companies doing business with Egypt and Jordan? Was the subject even raised within the PC?

5. Israel's response to suicide-bombers was a security barrier, a non-violent response to murder. What different response would have pleased the PC?

6. Because the Palestinians engage in murder, does the PC intend to boycott Palestinian products also?

7. Do you believe that Arafat is a real partner for peace? If so, kindly explain the 50 tons of armaments and ammunition on the *Karine-A*?

8. Wasn't Budapest militarily occupied by the Soviets in 1955 and Prague in 1968? What actions did the PC take at that time? Inasmuch as the former Soviet Union occupied all of Eastern Europe from 1945 to 1989, what steps were then taken by the PC to divest from companies doing business with the former Soviet Union? Can you name one?

9. Why does the PC align itself with the Palestinians – led by a dictatorship which has used women and children to create a culture of death and has intentionally targeted civilian women and children – rather than the Israelis, who flourish in a democratic culture built on desert sands, who heal all victims of terrorism in superior Israeli hospitals and who only want to be left alone?

I shall look for your answer.

PS: There was no reply from either Mr. Detterick or anyone else at the Presbyterian Church.

October 4, 2004

To the Editor (NYT):

Michael Tarazi's anti-Israel Op-Ed suggesting a one-state solution articulates virtually every lie uttered about Israel in this conflict. Sentence after sentence, paragraph after paragraph, one stunning lie heaped upon another, the assault on the truth had a numbing effect.

But I have a few questions for Mr. Tarazi:

Contrary to your suggestion, Muslims and Arabs are citizens of Israel, are protected by Israeli law, and are members of the Knesset. How many Jews sit in the councils of any Arab country? If and when Israel's Arab population exceeds her Jewish population, into whose hands should the Jews place their lives and security? Will sacred Jewish sites be destroyed and replaced with mosques, as has already happened in Palestinian-controlled West Bank cities? Palestinians regularly earn a living working in Israel. How many Jews are welcome to work in Gaza, Ramallah, Nablus or Jenin?

You aver that the Palestinians are being forced to accept "a one-state solution." Wasn't the PA offered at Camp David and Taba its own state with over 96% of the West Bank, all of Gaza and a shared capital in Jerusalem? Why was war the Palestinian reply to that offer?

You refer to the "uncomfortable reality" that Israel and the Palestinians already live together. You call that living? Will you still insist that the West Bank be *Judenrein* and that Jews will not have the right to worship at holy sites in the West Bank?

Can you identify a single terrorist group that has been disarmed or disbanded by the Palestinian Authority?

Mr. Tarazi's suggestion that a one-state solution offers Israel the opportunity to live in peace with the Palestinians recalls the same sickening refrain we heard 60 years ago that *arbeit macht frei*.

For the Record

October 11, 2004

To the Editor (NYT):

If anything could be more disturbing than the events at the school in Beslan last month, it has to be the announcement of Russian Deputy Foreign Minister Alexander Alexeyev that Russia will continue to assist Iran in its development of nuclear power. This is all the more remarkable since it is now common knowledge that the Chechans received assistance from al-Qaida in the planning and execution of the Beslan massacre. It does not require a degree from the Kennedy School at Harvard to understand that with Iran's acquisition of nuclear weapons terrorists with nuclear weapons are a certainty. And who, besides the Arabs, will be the beneficiaries of the transfer of nuclear armaments? Al-Qaida? The Chechan rebels, perhaps.

Perhaps Russia will complete an $800 million deal to build a nuclear reactor at Bushehr in southern Iran; an act, not of appeasement, but of cosmic greed and hubris which by definition will have consequences well beyond Mr. Putin's limited imagination. The Russian president would do well to heed the warning of the Italian poet Dante: "Abandon all hope, ye who enter." If only Mr. Putin were that prescient. It is not too late for Mr. Putin to stop feeding the beast that would turn on and consume his countrymen.

Israel and the Palestinians – What the Media Aren't Telling You

October 14, 2004

To the Editor (NYT):

Regarding last month's events in Beslan, we surely witnessed the tragedy of terrorism visited upon innocents. Unfortunately, the terrorists aren't done yet; we haven't even seen the end of Act I.

The problem isn't Iraq, Afghanistan, Syria or even the Saudis. The problem is Iran, and right under President Bush's nose – on his watch – the Iranians have developed a delivery system (the Shihab-3 ICBM) and will shortly have a nuclear weapon. While our troops were sent looking in foxholes for Saddam – and God knows where for weapons which had already been secreted to Syria – Iran is going nuclear with the assistance of France and Russia. Let there be no mistake that Iran will designate and arm terrorists as its battlefield proxy. The Chechan terrorists who received aid and technology from al-Qaida will be armed to the teeth. Then, somewhere in Europe, Israel or the United States, a major city will become a mass grave and a mere memory to be revisited only in photographs and films.

When Iran does have a nuclear weapon, it is questionable whether our president or that of any European country will tackle Iran. Rather, it may well fall to Israel to save Western civilization.

Saddam Hussein was thought to be easy and that's probably why Bush went into Iraq. Iran, especially a well-armed and nuclear Iran, is another kettle of fish. Had President Bush not squandered America's enormous prestige, good will and diplomatic strength (not to mention post-9/11 sympathy), he might have been able to persuade France and Russia not to create a nuclear power in a radical Islamic state that daily urges the death of America. That is the principle failure of his administration and, likely, his bequest to America. Everything else in the presidential campaign – the economy, gay rights, the Brady bill, etc. – is mere background music.

For the Record

October 11, 2004

To the Editor (Newsday):

Upon learning of Yasser Arafat's death, I thought of Lord Richmond's words at the end of *Richard III* when, standing over the tyrant's body, he said, "The bloody dog is dead."

Yet, realizing that I might appear ungrateful, I recalled the words of Mark Twain who, upon learning of the death of a particularly corrupt politician, said "I did not attend his funeral, but I did send a note of approval."

November 18, 2004

To the Editor (NYT):

While it is true that Arafat left his people empty-handed, their future is still firmly within their own grasp. If the Palestinians want peace, all they need to do is say so with their feet. If there is a "peace" faction among the Palestinians, now would be a good time to make themselves known.

Shall we see more rioting in the streets of Gaza? Shall we continue to hear calls for the destruction of Israel? Will their children still be taught to become suicide-bombers to kill Jews? Or will the culture of hate and death evolve toward civilization? Peace has always been within reach. With the death of Arafat, they can now show the world what they really want. Thus it is; thus it has always been.

For the Record

November 18, 2004

To the Editor (JP):

So Palestinian President Mahmoud Abbas is going to prohibit the public display of weapons? I laughed so hard I almost choked. What's he going to do? Go house to house with a big truck and a loudspeaker? Next, I suppose he'll institute a National Brotherhood Week, or maybe build a Holocaust Museum in Nablus.

Israel and the Palestinians – What the Media Aren't Telling You

December 2, 2004

Dear Chancellor Herman
[University of Illinois at Urbana-Champaign]:

It is sad to learn that two years after your school's paper published a blood libel against Israelis, it does so again. Mr. Danavi's piece contained serious misstatements of fact of such a nature as to bespeak a lack of interest in accuracy and strongly suggest invidious intent against Israel, and perhaps more.

By way of example, the charge that Prime Minister Sharon vowed to kill every Palestinian baby has been shown to be false. Miriam Sobh wrote the same blood libel two years ago in your paper; she issued an apology. The *Daily Illini* knows of the falsity of that statement, yet published the libel again. Why is that?

Second, Mr. Danavi baldly states that Prime Minister Sharon was found guilty of war crimes by the Israeli courts. This, too, is entirely false. No Israeli has been found guilty of war crimes in any court of any country, and to say otherwise is another blood libel. In fact, Lebanese militiamen killed the people in Sabra and Shatila. Christians kills Muslims and the Jews get blamed. This is fairly typical of negligent journalism, if not outright malice.

Other examples abound, but the above make the point. It is not sufficient to print "Letters to the Editor" pointing out the errors. What is required is a mechanism to insure against the publication of false statements, particularly those that poison the minds of your readers. So I ask: Is there a mechanism in place to prevent a third occurrence of this prejudice and incitement? If so, the current mechanism failed. And if not, why not?

Were we not dealing with so egregious a fault, it would be easy to pass it off to immaturity and youthful zeal. But the publication of a blood libel must carry consequences beyond publication of an apology. Journalistic integrity and standards are, after all, the editor's responsibility. I therefore suggest that the DI's editor be fired.

This breach of those standards should have consequences indicative of your office taking this matter seriously.

For the Record

December 20, 2004

To the Editor (NYT):

Scott Atran's suggestion (Op-Ed, 12/16/04) that Hamas "is willing to listen and wants to give democracy a chance" is symptomatic of what George Will correctly called the West's "inexhaustible obsequiousness."

Mr. Atran's belief in Hamas's willingness to entertain an "indefinite *hudna*" rests, he admits, upon Israel's willingness to "withdraw to pre-1967 borders, approve a right of return for Palestinian refugees, release long-term prisoners and raze the wall being built in the West Bank." In other words, Hamas will stop killing Israelis if Israel first commits suicide. This is not news, nor is it particularly insightful commentary. It is a pathetic attempt to put a happy face on terrorism and to justify murder. It is logic divorced from common sense and morality.

January 4, 2005

To the Editor:

Re: "Abbas: Fight against Zionist Enemy to Continue." It is not surprising that in campaigning for president, Mahmoud Abbas has picked up the Arafat/terrorist banner and affirms that the fight against the "Zionist enemy" will continue. He is, after all, just a politician looking for votes and he will say what is necessary to be elected.

Nevertheless, these are the words he will have to live with after the elections. If he is sincere in this desire for peace with Israel – something still very much in issue – how will the people who elected him respond when he tells them to end suddenly the armed struggle he openly calls for? This has always been a problem for those who preach the "hate your neighbor" philosophy: how to preserve your credibility after an about-face.

Rhetoric has a price. In this case, however, I suspect that it will be the Israelis, rather than the Palestinians, who will be asked to pay for Abbas's rhetoric.

For the Record

January 12, 2005

To the Editor:

I found it curious that Kofi Annan has decided to create a registry of Palestinian damage claims against Israel for the construction of the security fence. Secretary Annan stands at the forefront of the fight for universal civil rights.

Nevertheless, I do wonder why the United Nations and its secretary-general have failed to seek justice for the thousands of Israeli victims of Palestinian violence, among them: the 21 children murdered in a Ma'alot schoolhouse in 1974 by PLO terrorists disguised in Israeli army fatigues; the 28 killed and 140 injured in Netanya during a 2002 Passover seder; the 16 men, women and children killed in Be'er Sheva by double suicide-bombers last year; and the slaughter of pregnant Tali Hatuel and her four daughters. Perhaps it is an oversight.

Israel and the Palestinians – What the Media Aren't Telling You

January 26, 2005

To the Editor (Spectator in UK):

Your essay comparing the events at Jenin with the genocides of Auschwitz and Rwanda, beyond being irresponsible and reckless, crosses the lines of ignorance and bigotry. It is the anti-Semitism in Britain's mainstream media that has contributed heavily to a 50% increase in overt acts of Jew-hatred in 2004 over the numbers of 2003. This grotesque distortion suggests that either your editors were asleep at the switch or, more painfully, concurred with the author. Either way, your credibility is on a life-support system.

Moreover, for you to have published such a nasty article during the week commemorating the liberation of Auschwitz was simply mean and insensitive; more becoming the young heir to the House of Windsor than the longest continuously published English-speaking magazine in the world.

The late Adlai Stevenson – who died walking the streets of London – once said that credibility is to a journalist what virtue is to a lady, except a newspaper can always print a retraction. What are you going to do?

For the Record

February 3, 2005

To the Editor:

The arrest of a 15-year-old suicide-bomber tells us a few things: First, the Palestinian culture of death is alive and well. Even if the boy didn't know what he was carrying, the Palestinians are still ready to sacrifice their children to kill Israelis. Second, Abbas has not prevailed on the terrorists to call a truce, hudna or cease-fire. Suicide-bombers are readily deployed and Kassam rockets continue to be fired at Jewish settlements both in and out of Gaza. The alleged deployment of the Palestinian "security force" is a charade. Third, any so-called lull in violence is no more than playing possum. Whether Abbas cannot, or will not, control the terrorists is irrelevant, because it comes to the same thing. And in either case the bottom line is the same: no security for Israel. Back to "square one"? No. Back to ground zero.

Caroline Glick, one of the most astute and respected commentators on the Middle East wrote an essay "Return of the Peace Mongers" in which she addressed the proposed disengagement from Gaza and the consequences that would portend for Judea and Samaria. She was kind enough to respond to my e-mail.

Date: 8 Feb 2005

From: Caroline Glick

I think that if we could get Judea and Samaria for Gaza it would be a fair trade, but the point is that we are also ceding them. So we are enabling the formation of a terror zone in Gaza like Afghanistan and we are also moving along the garden path that will lead to Palestinian sovereignty over Judea and Samaria.

Best,
Caroline

I replied:

Dear Caroline,

Subject to a number of caveats, I have no problem letting the Arabs have Gaza back. Israel gains nothing in retaining possession of this sewer. Keep the fence up, patrol it, protect against tunnels and let the Arabs build their own paradise in Gaza as Israel did on the sands of the Negev. My primary concern with the disengagement is its unilateral nature. To leave without a substantial *quid pro quo* for, say, Judea and Samaria, will be a huge psychological victory for the terrorists. And this is to say nothing of the likelihood that Gaza will become a terrorist haven, which raises serious security issues to be sure.

Regarding Judea and Samaria, my misgivings are at an existential level. There is no question but that "Palestine" would become a base and an incubator for terrorism. The question will be: how much terrorism from the Palestinians will Israel suffer before the IDF is required to reenter Gaza, Nablus or Ramallah as it did in Jenin?

Moreover, given Russia's desire to play a major role in the Middle East, it would come as no surprise to see the Palestinians use part of the $320 million American loan to purchase "defensive" missiles and other armaments from Russia, Syria, North Korea or Iran.

Not to belabor the point, the so-called "road map" is wishful thinking. As you quite correctly point out, Abbas has taken no concrete steps to dismantle the terrorist networks. Remarkably, he will invite them to join the PA security forces if they sign a promise not to engage in terrorism! Didn't we travel this road before at Oslo?

The objections to turning over Judea and Samaria are too numerous to list here. What we are witnessing is the obvious prelude to events which will later be described as "unforeseen." And then God alone will be able to help us if my vision of a Palestinian state is on point.

Thank you for giving us the benefit of your thoughts.

February 24, 2005

To the Editor (NYT):

Your editorial ("Mr. Sharon's Giant Step") does Prime Minister Sharon, in particular, and the Israelis, in general, a disservice. The very first sentence sets the tone, opining your weariness "of any moves by the Israeli government to further consolidate land it seized after the 1967 war without negotiations with the Palestinians." Israel did not "seize" land following the Six Day War. It paid for those lands with the blood of its children in a defensive war initiated by its "neighbor" states and was forced to deploy the IDF there to provide security for Israel's citizens, Arab and Jewish. The consequence of the 1967 war was not a land grab and to suggest otherwise lacks any historical or factual basis.

As for "negotiations with the Palestinians," it is worth recalling that prior to the Six Day War every square inch of the "occupied" territories had been under the sovereignty of either Egypt, Jordan or Syria. Indeed, Egypt refused to take Gaza back and issued its three famous "no"s four months later in Khartoum. Jordan subsequently washed its hands of the West Bank Palestinians.

Israel tried to negotiate with the Arabs, who responded by turning their backs, not just on the Israelis, but also on their fellow Arabs.

For the Record

February 24, 2005

To the Editor (Toronto):

I am compelled to write about your Op-Ed columnist Eric Margolis. While his columns are published as "opinion," it seems to me that a paper of your caliber and reputation would require factual evidence before publishing invective and false charges. Mr. Margolis, it seems, has repeatedly expressed his anti-Israel opinions, which he is entirely entitled to hold. However, when he advances in your newspaper incendiary opinions having no basis in fact, he demeans himself, your paper and your paper's readers.

By way of example, just this month, his suggestion that Arafat was poisoned by the Israelis had absolutely no facts to back it up. It is noteworthy that the French doctors who treated Arafat specifically ruled out poisoning. Had Arafat been poisoned, one could expect to hear his widow screaming that charge at the top of her own anti-Semitic lungs. She didn't.

Likewise, his 1998 report that Israelis were trying to develop a bomb that would kill Arabs and spare Jews crossed all lines of known science and evidenced the poison in his own mind. Mr. Margolis is – outside the world of the anti-Israel crowds – a disgrace to his profession and your newspaper.

Perhaps Mr. Margolis should find another line of work – although I feel confident he would have no trouble finding employment at Al-Jazeera.

March 13, 2005

To the Editor (NYT):

I believe your editorial "Hizbullah and the Cedar Revolution" (March 13, 2005) is far wide of the mark. Hizbullah has decided to join the Lebanese political fracas not out of any sense of altruism, but because it enjoys such broad support it doesn't have to shed its own blood to rule Lebanon. This is not a case of a tiger changing its stripes, but rather merely theatrically purring for the Lebanese electorate. Once the Trojan Horse legitimately acquires power within the Lebanese government, Hizbullah will rightfully claim to be a "representative government" and thus trump all aces held by America and Europe. Hizbullah will then be free to crush its opponents with a ferocity all too familiar in the Middle East.

The problem with Hizbullah isn't its *modus operandi*, but rather its very character. Those who believe that Hizbullah will ever disarm are making a monumental misjudgment. Hizbullah will have the Lebanese on their knees as surely as Priam found himself before Achilles. Only where Achilles showed mercy, Hizbullah intends treachery.

For the Record

March 24, 2005

To the Editor (Newsday):

I must take exception to your editorial ("Mideast Contradiction", 3/24/05) bemoaning the expansion of the Israeli city of Ma'ale Adumim (population 30,000) by a mere 11.6% as "counter to efforts to erase the settlement issue as an obstacle to resolving the Israel-Palestine conflict."

Settlements would not even be an issue were it not for the Palestinian desire to make the West Bank *Judenrein*, i.e., to ethnically cleanse their proposed nation of all Jews. It is one thing to say that the Palestinians should have a nation in the West Bank, and quite another to say that Jews may not live there. Yet, that is the logical conclusion of the demand that Israel cease developing existing cities and settlements.

Or, to put the shoe on the other foot, suppose Israel proposed that no Arabs be permitted to live in Jerusalem or Haifa. This is no different from the Palestinian desire that Jews should not be allowed to live in Judea and Samaria. Sauce for the goose.

The suggestion that the issue of settlements should await final negotiations leaves open an issue that should not even be on the table; i.e., the right of Jews to live in Gaza, Judea and Samaria. It is important, and you quite rightfully acknowledge, that Ma'ale Adumim will be absorbed by Israel. Nothing seems to burn the Palestinian leadership so much as the thought of Jews on their landscape. It is that attitude – rather than an 11.6% growth of a Jewish city – which poses the more serious obstacle to peace.

Israel and the Palestinians – What the Media Aren't Telling You

March 29, 2005

To the Editor (JP):

The introduction of SA-7 Strella anti-aircraft missiles into Gaza from Egypt doesn't just cross a red line. It eloquently points to the same question that has been begged ever since Abbas campaigned to lead the PA: What do Abbas and the Palestinians really want?

What becomes clearer with each passing day and death is that the intifada and terrorism are far from over. Hamas leaders announce boldly that they are rearming and will take up arms again at a time of their choosing if Israel doesn't get out of all of Judea and Samaria. Kassam rockets are being made in Jenin and who knows where else. The official Palestinian Authority media continue to incite against Israel and PM Qurei is ready to push the button over E-1. All of this with Egypt's complicity.

And how is Abbas going to dismantle the terrorist network? By placing its jailed henchmen in the Palestinian Authority's security forces! Abbas has destroyed not a single terrorist cell and he long ago acknowledged that he would not use force to disarm them. The thought that there is peace around the corner would be laughable were it not for all the bloodshed that awaits us.

We already know what is in the Trojan Horse and yet Israel is urged to welcome it into Gaza, Judea and Samaria. These SA-7 Strella anti-aircraft missiles are just the beginning. News that Israel will abandon the Philadelphi Corridor surely gladdened the heart of Abbas. Sharon and Peres aren't relying on the fox to protect the chicken coop; they are placing the fox directly *in* the chicken coop.

What do the Palestinians want? Precisely what they have sought from Day One: the destruction of Israel. Arafat isn't dead. He's just put on a suit and told America and Europe what they want to hear. There is simply no evidence to the contrary. Sharon knows what's going on and hopefully he's too smart not to know what's coming. The question now is what can Sharon do to prevent the next intifada.

For the Record

April 2, 2005

To the Editor:

Re: "Abbas Starts Security Shake-Up," President Abbas's idea of a security shake-up is to start rolling some higher-up heads. That has the same smell of insincerity as that which rang hollow when Claude Reins urged in *Casablanca*: "Major Strasser has been shot. Round up the usual suspects." The problem is that the PA has no security system to speak of; much less one capable of maintaining order.

Insofar as Israel is concerned, Mr. Abbas could start cleaning up his act by refusing to hire killers. Contrary to reasonable expectations, jail time in an Israeli prison has become the *sine qua non* for entry into the PA security forces. That, however, is likely to change as Hamas introduces itself into the political system in the upcoming elections. Then, one need not have been in an Israeli jail to join the Palestinian police – membership in a gang with the blood of children on its hands will be sufficient.

Israel and the Palestinians – What the Media Aren't Telling You

May 13, 2005

To the Editor (JP):

I was both a little saddened and chagrined to read that a Palestinian student, Rami Daas, 26, had been kidnapped from his room in Mosul, Iraq. A plea for his release was even made by Palestinian Authority Prime Minister Qurei.

This is new territory for the Palestinians. Since they consistently ally themselves with Israel's enemies, they rarely find themselves looking down the barrel of an AK-47. Young Daas had recently undergone brain surgery and is on medication. One can only hope that his captors will find it in their hearts to release him unharmed and spare Daas and his family any further anguish.

While the Daas family and PM Qurei are asking for mercy perhaps they will put in a kind word for Ron Arad. Or not.

For the Record

May 16, 2005

To the Editor (NYT):

Re: "Give Palestinian Police Arms." Given President Abbas's position that he will not allow Palestinian security forces to fire on Palestinians lest that lead to a civil war, it is disingenuous that he demanded weapons and ammunition for his policemen to "operate normally." If the police cannot use their guns against Palestinians, then against whom do you suppose these weapons would be used?

Not so long ago, Palestinian police armed with Israeli-supplied rifles were shooting at the IDF. At riots in Nablus, Jenin and Gaza, there was no report of a single Palestinian – armed or unarmed – making any effort to restore peace.

The fact that the Palestinian Authority is armed with Israel's consent only underscores the immense hubris we are witnessing as Sharon leaves Gaza without a *quid pro quo*.

June 2, 2005

To the Editor (JP):

Re: "Would I Have Sent my Son to his Death?" To the parents of Mohammed al-Nadi, the 15-year-old who was arrested trying to carry out a suicide-bombing mission at the Hawara checkpoint south of Nablus: I can understand your anger at those who sent him on this mission. It was both cruel and criminal to have done so.

But I have some questions: You say that your 15-year-old son was incapable of "differentiating between good and bad." If that is so, why did you fail, over a period of 15 years, to teach him such fundamental values? If he was unable to differentiate between good and bad, how did he know it was alright to kill Jews, but not Arabs? Was he taught to hate before he could think? How did he come to believe that if he killed Jews, he would die a martyr and go to heaven? What did you teach him about the sanctity of life? What did you tell him when he saw his people cheer as Iraqi Scud missiles flew overhead toward Tel Aviv? Were you cheering yourself?

Did you not know what he was learning in school? Did you not hear the same anti-Semitic rhetoric on your TVs and radios that your son heard? What did you do about it? What did you think would come of such an "education?"

Terrorists using your children to kill our children didn't just start last week. As you watched for years as dozens of youths were being used to kill Israelis, did you do anything to protest such a cruel practice? Or did this suddenly strike you as wrong only after your own son had been recruited?

Have you even once raised your voice in opposition to the murder of women and children? Did you organize a demonstration or a rally against this practice? Your son was taught to hate the Israelis all his life. What did you think he was going to become?

Yours is a culture of death. But only you Palestinians can change that. Do you want to? Do you love your son more than you hate the Israelis?

For the Record

June 3, 2005

To the Editor (NYT):

Your comment that, "It seems odd to bemoan the absence of democracy when Palestinians held a free and fair presidential election in January [and] it will become harder for any Israeli government to argue they shouldn't have a state within which to practice it" misses the mark. The problem isn't a democratically elected government. The problem is a democratically elected terrorist government. You will recall the electoral success of the National Socialists in 1930s Germany and, recently, of Hizbullah in Lebanon. More than free elections is required to form a democracy.

There seems to be little doubt that Hamas will score significant victories and, if so, will likely be given more than just a "seat at the table." If democratically elected, who could deny them? The dilemma of an "Arab democracy" would then come crashing down on the United States. Nevertheless, it is important to recall that both Fatah and Hamas have yet to revoke their covenants to destroy Israel.

And yet, how could anyone seriously expect the Israeli government – under Sharon or anyone else – to negotiate with a government dedicated to her destruction? But that is, in fact, entirely likely to happen.

Hopefully, Prime Minister Sharon is too smart to be drawn into such a no-win situation. But we should be prepared to stand on the principle that terrorist's have no place in government, even if democratically elected. It may very well come to that.

June 8, 2005

To the Editor:

Re: "Hamas Ready for Talks with US and Europe." Hamas spokesman Ghazal's willingness to negotiate with the United States and Europe suggests that he has been asleep for the past 67 years. It is not 1938, the US is not led by Neville Chamberlain, and Israel is not a weak and helpless Czechoslovakia.

Mr. Ghazal should also bear in mind that Europe's historical practice of appeasement and her thinly veiled anti-Semitism make Europe's intentions irrelevant. Israel can never again trust her children to the Europeans.

Insofar as America is concerned, Mr. Ghazal should by now be convinced that it is as yet unlikely that President Bush would negotiate with terrorists – even if democratically elected in the upcoming elections.

If Hamas has anything to say, it must first disarm and destroy its military bases. And after that, there is still only one address from which to negotiate: The Prime Minister's Office in the undivided capital of Israel, Jerusalem.

For the Record

June 21, 2005

To the Editor:

Re: "Sharon and Abbas Set to Meet Today as Violence Continues." Your article creates the misimpression that there is a moral equivalence, and therefore, responsibility, for the escalation of violence in Gaza and the West Bank. Such is not the case. On January 19, 2005, a 16-year-old Palestinian boy carrying five pipe bombs was intercepted by the IDF. A 21-year-old Islamic Jihad fugitive was arrested for planning a suicide-bombing attack only weeks after Israel released him from jail as a "sign of good faith" and to bolster President Abbas.

In fact, more than 50 Palestinians under the age of 18, mostly with pipe bombs, have been arrested for involvement in terrorist activities in the past five and a half months.

I might add that the 21-year-old woman you identify as intending to kill 40 to 50 Israelis said she was not going to do it at the Soroka Hospital in Be'er Sheva, where she receives treatment. She planned to do it at another Israeli hospital.

Israel and the Palestinians – What the Media Aren't Telling You

July 2, 2005

To the Editor:

PA President Abbas's invitation to Hamas to join his cabinet confirms some of our worst fears about the "new" Palestinian Authority: Abbas's goals are no different than were Arafat's – he wears a suit instead of the kefiyah – and Israel will be told to negotiate her life with those who demand her death, principally Hamas, the most unrepentant of murderers among the Palestinian terrorists. With a seat in the PA's cabinet, Abbas seeks to bestow upon Hamas a level of credibility and respectability well beyond that normally given to a band of killers.

Unfortunately, with Hamas growing in political strength and Abbas losing ground on the Palestinian street, this marriage of treachery and blood-lust comes as no surprise. This is particularly so with Palestinian elections poised to give Hamas both credibility and power. Abbas had to bring Hamas into the fold.

It remains to be seen whether America and the Europeans forget that this group, once led by the murderous Rantisi and Yassin, was responsible for some of the most heinous murders of Israel's civilians. As Shakespeare wrote, "Some rise by sin; others by virtue fall." Hamas's star is ascending.

This would also be the Bush administration's first real test of democratization in the Middle East – how to respond to a government that bestows legitimacy upon terrorists.

The first obligation of the Palestinian Authority under the Road Map was the destruction of the terrorist network. Not only did Abbas try to co-opt rather than destroy the terrorists, his offer to Hamas is a direct broadside against the Road Map. The message from Ramallah could not be clearer: the Palestinian Authority does not want a two-state solution and it is unwilling or unable (which amounts to the same thing) to remove the terrorists.

Israel would do well to send a strong message to the PA that she will not negotiate with terrorists, even under color of legitimacy. Abbas's offer to Hamas leaves the Road Map dead in the water, and so Israel must create its own facts on the ground.

Sharon should declare that the disengagement from Gaza is called off, not merely postponed. Canceling the disengagement gives Sharon the rare opportunity to kill two birds with one stone: First, he can shore up his crumbling support in Israel. The IDF, Shin Bet and most of the military/security experts do not agree that peace can come from leaving Gaza, which only rewards terrorism and is appeasement. Second, he sends a strong message to the Palestinians and terrorists that they were wrong to think Israel can be bullied and bruised into surrender. That would be a message the Palestinians would understand.

July 15, 2005

To the Editor (NYT):

Your editorial "Aimless in Gaza" (7/15/05) bluntly and erroneously places the blame for both the anarchy in Gaza and Mr. Abbas's declining popularity on Prime Minister Sharon. It is important not to confuse cause and effect. The anarchy in Gaza is the result of Mr. Abbas's refusal to create an effectual security force and to destroy Hamas, Islamic Jihad, Al Aksa Martyrs Brigade, etc. Had Mr. Abbas made even the slightest effort to do so, the situation in Gaza could still be dangerous but well short of the outright anarchy we witness daily.

As for Mr. Abbas's second problem – declining popular support – this, too, is the consequence of his resolute failure to root out Fatah corruption and to provide leadership and security for his own people.

It is Mr. Abbas, not Mr. Sharon, who is responsible for the horrible conditions that presently exist, and which will only deteriorate, in Gaza. One way or the other, Mr. Abbas must go.

For the Record

July 21, 2005

To the Editor:

There is talk in London of appeasing the Muslim terrorists who have attacked, not just the Underground, but the very essence of English society. It is quite easy to explain: "Please just leave us alone. We'll do whatever you want, but I want my wife/husband/children to be safe." Certainly understandable sentiments drawn in blood by fear and terror. But that approach will not solve their problem and will likely lead to more bloodshed.

To be sure, this is a war. It is a war of cultures, not between competing ideas in university debate clubs, in the newspapers, on the BBC, or even over a pint of ale in the local pub. It is a military war between cultures of freedom, democracy, education, respect and inclusion against a fanatical religious culture that teaches hatred, death and intolerance. This is the radical Muslim version of the Crusades of the 12th and 13th centuries; only instead of Christian warriors off to liberate Jerusalem from Islam, these Islamic murderers have also brought the fight to Western civilization.

There is no easy way out of this. It must be confronted head on with every tool allowed by law. The religious fanatics must be given no quarter, no respite, no hiding place, no comfort. We must not yield; we must not turn away from this deadly contest; we must not withdraw or retreat.

To those who think our freedom and values are negotiable, I refer you to the words of the great Churchill upon Chamberlain's return from Munich, "The prime minister has been given the choice between war and shame. He has chosen shame. He shall surely have war."

Israel and the Palestinians – What the Media Aren't Telling You

July 29, 2005

To the Editor (NYT):

Your editorial "Nourishing Palestinian Police" urging Israel to "stop blocking attempts to rebuild Palestinian security forces" fails to take into account recent history. The Palestinian security forces were decimated by Israel in 2002 – in the middle of the most recent intifada – because those forces failed to rein in rioting, mayhem and murder, and did themselves participate in the intifada. Israel cannot be faulted for refusing to arm the very people who try to kill her.

More recently, following the July 12 suicide bombing in Netanya, it was learned that part of that suicide mission was planned inside the police station in Tul Karm under the watchful eyes of the Palestinian security forces.

Furthermore, it is inaccurate to blame Israel's settlement policy for Palestinian anarchy in Gaza. This is particularly so as the settlements are being prepared for disengagement. Do you really think that after the disengagement Gaza will be restored to tranquility? We'll see.

Palestinian anarchy has less to do with the Israelis than with their own culture of death and the pervasive corruption of their leaders. To suggest otherwise is disingenuous.

August 16, 2005

To the Editor (JP):

It is alarming, but not really a surprise: Disengagement has just started, the dust hasn't even begun to settle and already the Palestinians are pushing for their next gift from Israel.

Palestinian pressure on Israel to go to final-status talks has already started to build. The Palestinians are talking "Jerusalem next!" and the United Nations is providing flags that say "Gaza today! The West Bank and Jerusalem tomorrow!" The Arabs are prepared to take control of Judea and Samaria and Jerusalem at this moment. These people are feeling their oats. They believe that nothing can stop them; certainly not the Israelis. And why not, since Sharon has served up Gaza on a silver platter and, to make the meal easier to digest, tore up the bill. After five years and thousands of dead and mutilated Israelis, the Arabs didn't have to do so much as return the remains of Ron Arad.

Meanwhile, in Gaza the settlers are still negotiating with the government; Palestinians are shooting at the settlers; Kassam rockets are still being fired into the Jewish neighborhoods; the Palestinian police stand by as death squads execute Palestinians in the street; and Secretary Rice is urging "contiguity" between Gaza and Judea and Samaria.

Somebody needs to call a time out. Complete the disengagement and then see what's left standing. There are mountains of work to accomplish immediately after the disengagement: housing, elections, security, jobs, infrastructure, disarmament of the militias, an end to wildfire anarchy and corruption, and on and on.

Before Israel does anything further, the Palestinians must put their house in order, if they can. Everything starts with the terrorist groups and anarchy. Unless Abbas can restore law and order in Gaza – overwhelmingly unlikely – the Palestinians are going nowhere if not down a black hole. And co-opting Hamas and Islamic Jihad into the security forces won't cut it.

The first taste of medicine is the most bitter; but taking on the terrorists is the Palestinian Authority's first order of business. It may cost Abbas his life, but if he fails in that test, life in Gaza and Judea and Samaria will deteriorate further, and, as difficult as that sounds, it is entirely possible.

For the Record

August 18, 2005

To the Editor (NYT):

I disagree with your editorial "Gaza Reality Check," which concludes that it's time "to give the Palestinians there a chance at a better life," thus placing upon the Israelis the blame for the misery in the Gaza Strip. The violence in Gaza is the direct consequence of the acts of the Palestinians.

It is inconsistent on the one hand to blame an Israeli army blockade with making crossing into Israel difficult, and then on the other hand acknowledge that these checkpoints were "set up in response to terrorist attacks" which you further acknowledge started during the intifada in 2000.

Everything Israel did in Gaza was for one of two purposes: to protect the Israeli settlers from Palestinian violence, or to prevent and intercept terrorist attacks aimed at Israel proper.

Israel and the Palestinians – What the Media Aren't Telling You

September 12, 2005

To the Editor (Newsday):

As Israel has completed its withdrawal from Gaza, the Palestinians have again revealed their true character. Within scant hours after the IDF had left, the Palestinians started to tear down and burn the remaining synagogues. Their delight was unconcealed. Indeed, even before the fires had died and the smoke cleared, the Palestinian president and a senior Hamas official defended destruction of the temples. Incredibly, Abbas declared that Israelis had left no synagogues behind in Gaza; only dilapidated buildings on the brink of collapse. Hamas spokesman Ismail Haniyeh sneered that his people "would not allow any Wailing Walls on our blessed land."

One must ask why this had to happen. The answer lies first in the fact that 1.4 million Arabs refused to live in peace with 8,000 Jews.

This past week, the Israelis asked Palestinian President Abbas if he would use his good offices to protect Jewish holy sites. Abbas refused. It is not that Abbas was incapable of protecting the sites. The Palestinian Authority's militias are armed and over 50,000 strong. To assign several thousand men to prevent defilement of a holy site would hardly have affected the chaos and anarchy running rampant in Gaza. The straight answer is that Mr. Abbas did not want to protect the synagogues and was more than content to let his fellow Palestinians have their way with them. Hatred is a strong unifier. And these are the very people with whom Israel is called upon to make peace and entrust with the protection of Judaism's holy sites in Judea, Samaria and Jerusalem?

When the Taliban announced that they were going to destroy the 800-year-old Buddhas in Afghanistan, world figures, including the Pope, urged them not to do so. And although their words fell on deaf ears, at least some effort was made to prevent that despicable act. But in Gaza? Nothing was done to protest or prevent the destruction of the Gaza synagogues. No one lifted a hand or, with the exception of President Bush, raised his voice against this perfidy.

In its creation of an apartheid Gaza, not one nation has stood up to condemn this ethnic cleansing. Not Britain, not France, not the United States, not the United Nations or the European Community. No one. It is worth remembering that Israel outlawed Meir Kahane's Kach Party, which argued for the extradition of all Arabs from Israel.

It was not enough that the Jews had left Gaza. The Palestinians had to destroy any evidence that Jews had even been there. And the rest of the world sat on their hands. Again.

Israel and the Palestinians – What the Media Aren't Telling You

September 21, 2005

To the Editor (NYT):

Secretary Rice's urging the Israelis to aid in the upcoming Palestinian elections ("Rice Urges Israel to Aid Palestinian Election" Sept. 21, 2005) underscores the very quagmire in which the Bush administration has found itself, in both fighting terrorism and trying to spread democracy in the Middle East. Israel knows, as apparently the secretary does not, that open and free elections in Gaza and Palestinian cities will result in numerous victories by terrorists, primarily Hamas. I have no doubt that the *Times* will then insist that Israel negotiate with a democratically elected terrorist government dedicated to her destruction.

You cannot marry terrorism and democracy. Participation by Hamas in the political process will no more moderate their behavior than did the participation of the National Socialists in Germany during the 1930s. Terrorists have no place in government, even if freely elected.

For the Record

September 23, 2005

To the Editor (NYT):

Thomas Friedman's Op-Ed ("Rooting for Bibi is Rooting for Israel") makes the same errors in judgment that have plagued Shimon Peres and his Labor Party for decades. And that is the assumption that, just because the Israeli public wants a peaceful two-state solution, so too do the Palestinians.

The impediment to a two-state solution is that there is nobody in the Palestinian camp with whom to make peace. Gaza is already in a state of anarchy, something already spreading to Palestinian cities in the West Bank. Abu Mazen is, at best, a figurehead, and Fatah is losing ground quickly to Hamas. Only Hamas, which insists on the death of Israel, sees its star rising.

Until there is a solid, widespread grassroots peace movement among the Palestinians, Israel lacks a genuine partner for peace. As matters now stand, Israel is the bridegroom waiting in vain at the altar.

September 28, 2005

To the Editor (NYT):

Your editorial ("Ariel Sharon's Choice: Israel or Likud?" 9/28/05) puts the onus for peace on Prime Minister Sharon's shoulders while making only parenthetical reference to the Palestinians. You urge Sharon to proceed with further disengagement and continue on "the path that Israel has to pursue if it ever expects to make peace with the Palestinians."

What you overlook is that the obstacle to peace is the Palestinian refusal to stop killing Israelis, and that Israel's withdrawal from Gaza would never have been necessary if 1.4 million Arabs could have lived in peace with 8,000 Israelis.

Even if Israel left the West Bank, what makes you think that millions of Palestinians would live in peace with five million Jews? This isn't about numbers. It is the mere existence of the Jews that has the Palestinians apoplectic.

Finally, if Gaza teaches us anything, it is that Israel has no partner for peace. It is Mr. Abbas's failure to resolutely take control of the streets that causes chaos and anarchy to metastasize in the Palestinian cities and continue to threaten Israelis, both Jewish and Arab.

For the Record

October 10, 2005

To the Editor (Newsday):

It is reported out of Norway that a teacher working at an adult education center there was directed in 2004 to stop wearing a Star of David because it "provokes the many Muslim students at the school." The head of the school said that the Star of David can be seen to represent the State of Israel and he is fearful of offending the school's Muslim students, citing immigrants from the Palestinian territories. The teacher, who is not Jewish, said the star is small (only 0.6 inches) and that he usually wears it under his T-shirt. It is, he says, his right. Curiously, Norway's education minister said last year that she had no intention of banning the wearing of hijabs in Norwegian public schools.

Perhaps it is to be expected that the Star of David should be a problem in the country from which is derived the word "quisling," referring to the Norwegian diplomat of that name who ruled Norway on behalf of the occupying Nazis during the Second World War. What is surprising is that the Norwegians have learned nothing from their past.

Let us put the shoe on the other foot and ask whether Norway would bar the Muslim Crescent for fear of provoking Jews whose countrymen had been murdered as a consequence of Muslim anti-Semitism. I doubt that such a ban would even be considered and all discussion would turn to demanding that the Jews learn to be tolerant of others. And so it falls to the government of Norway to protect those who wish to practice their religion in peace, and to punish those who would bring violence to those who do not share a particular theology.

The problem with appeasement is that it does not work, a lesson taught time and again in history…and sadly ignored. Once appeased, the offenders are emboldened to physical violence, be it a gang beating or desecration of religious sites. (France provides us with such an example.) Once the door of prejudice is opened even a crack, the seeds of hate are spread by the wind.

The Norwegian government must denounce religious prejudice and institute a program of zero-tolerance in fighting hatred.

October 14, 2005

To the Editor (JP):

I found it curious that the Palestinian Authority is pleased that its terrorists may be treated by Israel as prisoners of war. ("PA: Israel may Reconsider Status of Prisoners" 11 October 2005). PA Minister of Prisoner Affairs Sufian Abu Zaida explained that the prisoners had been acting on the instructions of the PLO "The entire PLO leadership is responsible for the prisoners," he explained.

Let us put that piece of data together with one other and see where it leads. When the International Court of Justice ruled that Israel could not construct the security fence, it was because the court found that the terrorists were not an aggressor state and, therefore, Israel had no right to invoke the doctrine of self-defense.

The PLO is a national liberation organization with functioning executive, legislative, police and security departments, and what passes in the Middle East for a judiciary.

If, as Minister Zaida argues, the terrorists are to be treated as POWs, then *a fortiori* they acted as part of a national militia; otherwise they would be mere criminals.

If the PLO wants its prisoners treated as POWs, and argues that the prisoners acted in an army under its direction and control, then Israel's security fence, even under the warped ruling of the ICJ, is a justifiable act of self-defense against terrorists of a national authority. POWs? Again, sauce for the goose.

For the Record

October 31, 2005

To the Editor (JP):

Were it not for the rampant anti-Semitism that has encircled the globe with renewed enthusiasm for the past several years, I would be surprised by the "no-sanctions" response to Iran's exhortation to "wipe Israel off the face of the Earth." This could otherwise easily be dismissed as the rantings of a mad man, a religious fanatic and a typical, anti-Semitic Middle East tyrant.

From the day the United Nations gave birth to the State of Israel, it has not once lifted a finger to protect that life. It is, therefore, unlikely that the General Assembly will entertain, much less pass, a motion to condemn Iran's criminally insane demand. And with the Russians still doing business with the Iranians, we've already been told that the Russian bear will veto any Security Council resolution against its client. So much for the United Nations.

Typically, the West is clucking its thick tongue as though that were a sufficiently stern warning that would focus Iran's sense of self-preservation. From Tony Blair's adjective-laced condemnation to Kofi Annan's suggestion that the Iranians work harder on their people skills, Iran has pretty much gotten a "get-out-of-jail-free" card.

This is no time for appeasement. Speeches will not do. Nor will threats to send them off to bed without dinner. Iran will soon represent the single greatest threat to world stability since the Third Reich. For decades she has called for Israel's destruction. Only now when she says it, we know that Iran has the missile technology – and soon enough a nuclear payload – to make good on its threat. Only a fool would play this game of Russian roulette to see if Iran is as good as its word.

What we need are people in the same mold as WWII General MacAuliffe who, surrounded at Bastogne by Nazis demanding his surrender, replied, "Nuts!" It's time for plain talk and serious sanctions. In the absence of an agreement – continuously verified by, not the UN, but a serious multinational committee of leading

Israel and the Palestinians – What the Media Aren't Telling You

physicists – not to produce weapons-grade uranium, a series of incentives should be presented to Iran. Start with a multinational declaration that Iran is *persona non grata*. (This may be merely name-calling, but it is a start, and certainly better than our current non-response.) Follow that promptly with a trade embargo overseen by someone the stature of a Paul Volker instead of UN sybarite Kofi Annan. Send an international fleet to seal off her ports. (Iran imports 40% of its gasoline). Call in all her international debt and freeze all financial accounts. Food and medicine could be bought only through a NATO oversight committee. Let them choke on their oil.

A nuclear Iran is too serious a threat to ignore any longer. We know what the Iranian leaders are, what they are capable of and want they aspire to. They must be stopped now. We have no right to expect the Israelis to pull our chestnuts out of the fire as they did for us with Iraq almost 27 years ago. The Iranians and radical Islam are world problems.

For the Record

November 16, 2005

To the Editor (Newsday):

Your editorial ("In Mideast, US is Needed" 11/15/05) quite correctly points out the need for America's presence in the negotiations between Israelis and Palestinians.

Yet it is important to understand why America is necessary to the equation: Without American pressure on the Palestinians to put their house in order, terrorism, corruption and anarchy will continue to contaminate all of Gaza and much of the West Bank.

The only positive steps taken have been those by the Israelis. Since Israel's unilateral disengagement from Gaza, Kassam rockets continue to fall on Sderot, Palestinian suicide-bombers continue to murder Israeli women and children, rabid anti-Semitism issues daily from the official Palestinian media like so much sewage, and Hamas, Islamic Jihad and Al Aksa Martyrs' Brigade do as they wish under the watchful eye of a duplicitous Palestinian president.

Nevertheless, and in spite of Palestinian paralysis, the Israelis are opening border crossings to permit Palestinian workers and products to cross into Israel, while still trying to maintain a proper level of security for its citizens, both Arab and Jewish.

Secretary Rice would do well to keep the pressure on…the Palestinians.

Israel and the Palestinians – What the Media Aren't Telling You

November 17, 2005

To the Editor (JP),

It came as neither a disappointment nor a surprise to read that hundreds, maybe a thousand, Gazans armed with rifles and rocket launchers marched openly in defiance of a PA directive not to display weapons in public. ("Palestinians Stage Mass Armed March" 17 November 2005) Anarchy is the *plat du jour* in Gaza. Marches, parades and other demonstrations of firepower are routine.

What is conspicuously absent anywhere among the Palestinian population is so much as the hint of a peace movement. Is there not a single Palestinian who sees the way of the Palestinian irredentists as an obituary? Is there not a single Palestinian with the courage to march in Ramallah with a sign reading "Stop the killing!"? Where are the mothers, wives and daughters supposedly imbued with nature's maternal instinct to preserve the lives of their children?

I'll tell you where they are: They are marching with Hamas; they are destroying the very greenhouses that would have put food on their tables and given jobs to hundreds; they take their children to mosques where their holy men spew hatred and urge murder; they are dressing their five-year-old sons to go to school and learn to hate Jews and carry explosives under their coats; and, they are at home at night watching TV hearing killers exhort their children to martyrdom.

They are preparing, while their children are in school, to tie explosives around their own waists so they can "arrive in paradise holding the skulls of seven Zionists;" they return from their daily chores to place explosives in a satchel they plan to explode at a checkpoint or, worse, in an Israeli hospital where Jewish doctors work day and night saving Palestinian children injured in accidents caused by their own people. They are in the streets giving interviews to Al-Jazeera bemoaning the fact that their son who killed 20 Jews with a suicide bomb wasn't carrying a nuclear bomb!

They are preparing for death instead of having the joy of watching their children grow up; instead of being there to hug, love and comfort their children.

They are preparing for death. The death of their parents, their husbands and wives, their sons and daughters, their friends and, of course, themselves.

Israel and the Palestinians – What the Media Aren't Telling You

December 7, 2005

To the Editor (JP):

The news that the International Red Cross is on the brink of admitting the Magen David Adom is good news. The bad news is that the Star of David will be replaced with a neutral red "crystal," within which Israel may have the option of placing the Star of David, *if* the host country agrees. The symbol of Judaism for millennia being relegated to an inferior status, Jews continue to be treated as *dhimmi*.

Let us be clear what this is about. First, it is not about providing medical care, which is what the IRC is supposed to do. It is not about the quality of care. No one seriously disputes that the Israelis provide the best medical care in the Middle East and, likely, Europe, Africa and Asia, and do so for Israelis and non-Israelis alike. This is about erasing us Jews. Denying us the same visibility, prominence and respect as Christian and Muslim nations enjoy. They may not be able to make us disappear, but they are doing their best to diminish our status, as well as visibility and, therefore, our very existence, in a hostile world. It is another arrow in the quiver of anti-Semitism directed at the symbol of the Jewish people.

That the symbol of our people receives such treatment is not surprising nor so disturbing as is the fact that Israelis, in a proportionate act of appeasement, actually agreed to it. We have become the 21st century equivalent of the *conversos* of the Spanish Inquisition. What monstrous forces of hubris are at work that we again, to use a familiar analogy, walk quietly to the gas chambers? Is membership in the IRC such a moral imperative that we should compromise our identity or the symbol of our essence? I simply don't understand.

For the Record

December 20, 2005

To the Editor:

Last week, it was disclosed that Palestinian police stationed at the Karni crossing in Gaza helped plan a terrorist bombing there. The policemen reportedly were going to allow the terrorists to detonate a large bomb at the crossing while it was being scanned by the IDF. The assault was also intended to include opening fire and throwing grenades. The scheme was derailed by alert IDF troops. (Curiously, none of the American or European media reported it.)

This isn't the first time the Palestinian police have been involved in the murder of Israelis – it happened at the police station in Ramallah in 2000, when two IDF reservists made a wrong turn on a road and were beaten to death – but the incident at Karni is the most recent and, therefore, the most important.

So, the question is: How can you expect peace when the Palestinian Authority's own police and security forces are participating in terrorism; this at the same time their president publicly calls for a *hudna*. Instead of being a solution, the Palestinian police and security forces are a serious part of the problem. Needless to say, Mr. Abbas knows full well what is going on and refuses to stop it, which for the future bodes even worse.

Here are the problems: Aside from the fact that Abbas doesn't have the muscle to disarm the terrorists, what's worse is that he doesn't want to. Abbas is trying to co-opt the terrorists into the Palestinian security forces. Giving guns and badges to criminals has never served the interests of law enforcement. Indeed, Abbas has no intention of dismantling the terrorist network. He has said so explicitly. He will not order his security and police forces to disarm, much less fire upon, fellow Palestinians.

The terrorists explicitly state that they will never give up their weapons. The Left opines that once Hamas enters the political arena, it will join the process. Wishful thinking. Hamas specifically and publicly refuted this and said it is not a political party. Of course, one could see how the National Socialists moderated when they joined the political process in 1930s Germany; or how Hizbullah has been sedated by its election to the Lebanese parliament.

It is worth noting that Hamas has recently been sitting at the knee of the notorious Muslim Brotherhood. Just this past weekend, prominent Hamas candidate Miriam Farhat – known as the "Mother of Martyrs" because she sent her three sons to die as suicide-bombers – met with Mehdi Akef, the Brotherhood's spiritual leader, who declared: "We will not recognize Israel...an alien entity in the region. We expect the demise of this cancer soon." For her part, Farhat said that Hamas's decision to participate in the parliamentary elections does not mean that the Islamic movement has abandoned the "military option." This unholy alliance has Fatah taking Prozac.

I believe that Abbas has no desire to live in peace with Israel; not under a two-state system or otherwise. I say this for a number of reasons, but primarily because of his position on terrorism. President Abbas condemns murder only because in his view it does not advance the Palestinian cause. It's bad publicity. That's all. He has never condemned terrorism on any moral basis. In other words, he tells his Palestinians that murdering Israeli civilians is the right idea, but this isn't the right time to do it. Neither Abbas nor anyone in the Palestinian community has condemned murder because it is wrong.

Nor should it go unstated that Abbas refuses to hold the terrorists accountable for their acts. Indeed, the terrorists do his bidding as he, with a wink and crocodile tears, denies complicity and the power to interfere. Abbas's hollow condemnation of cold-blooded murder rings with the same sincerity as Hitler's declaration that Czechoslovakia was his last territorial demand. Terrorism could never have reached its current level without Abbas's knowledge and consent. He refuses to take on the terrorist militias for the very reason that they act as his alter ego.

Let's also take a brief look at what Abbas has done to encourage terrorism. Al-Moayed Bihokmillah Al-Agha murdered five Israelis in a suicide-bombing at the Rafah crossing in late 2004. When that crossing was recently reopened, the Palestinian Authority named it "in honor of Shahid [martyr] Al-Agha." Not to be overlooked are the soccer tournaments named in honor of the terrorist who murdered 30 people at a Passover seder at the Park Hotel in Netanya in 2002, and a girl's high school named after a female terrorist who murdered 36 Israelis.

Most recently, on the very day that a suicide-bomber murdered five Israelis at a shopping mall, again in Netanya, PA President Abbas approved financial assistance – a monthly stipend of the not insubstantial sum of $250 for the families of suicide-bombers – and thus encouraged those who murder Israelis. Money has also been set aside for families of terrorists in Israeli jails and those wounded in attacks on Israelis. Instead of confronting the terrorists, Abbas is actually paying them a bounty for dead Israelis. Today, the going rate for families of suicide-murderers is $3,000 a year. The president of the Palestinian Authority has put a bounty on our heads. It's time to acknowledge that Abbas himself is an integral part of the terrorist machine.

There are many indications that the Palestinians don't want peace, but none much stronger than the fact that Hamas is on the brink of gaining control of the Palestinian National Council in a democratic vote. Note that Hamas claims the credit for forcing Israel out of Gaza and remains dedicated to destroy Israel. It has not wavered in that goal one iota. Whether or not Hamas's claim is true is irrelevant. That is the perception, and in the Middle East perception is often more important than reality. It alters the way people think.

Hamas has gained the trust and sympathy of the Palestinian people, and if the people are going to vote for Hamas it makes no distinction between its military and civic functions. A vote for Hamas is a vote for the destruction of Israel. There is no way to get around it. Add up the above and one conclusion leaps to mind: There's no one on the other side who wants a peaceful two-state solution.

As I see it, Israel has three choices: one, do nothing; two, negotiate with the PA after its elections; or, three, take matters into her own hands. The status quo is unacceptable for a number of reasons. Next, one does not negotiate with people whose only goal is to see you dead; unless, of course, you're Peretz or Peres. In any event, the Bush Road Map is tenuously tethered to life-support, and when the Palestinian elections are over and Hamas has "a seat at the table" it will be stone-cold dead.

That leaves the third choice: In a hostile world, Israel must take matters of its security into her own hands. The first obligation of a nation is to protect its citizens. The only reasonable way to do so is to keep the Gazan and West Bank Palestinians out of Israel in a manner that doesn't hurt Israel. Israel has started to do so with the construction of the security fence. It must be completed and Israel free to respond militarily to missiles over, and tunnels under, the barrier. Israel must be free to establish her own borders – wherever they need to be – and the Palestinians be damned. It won't be popular in Europe, the UN or even in America. But it will save innocent lives, and for now that's my overriding concern.

If there were ever a good time for Palestinian supporters of peaceful coexistence to make themselves known, it is now. It would go a long way in restoring hope. We're waiting; but we won't be sitting on our hands.

For the Record

December 23, 2005

To the Editor (NYT):

I can well understand the Palestinian complaints about having to wait hours to pass through an Israeli checkpoint ("Israel is Easing Barrier Burden, But Palestinians Still See a Border," 12 Dec. 2005). I have a solution: stop sending Palestinians to kill Israelis. No murders, no fence. No fence, no checkpoints.

As for their other concern that the fence looks like a border, to paraphrase an old saw: Good borders make good neighbors.

Israel and the Palestinians – What the Media Aren't Telling You

December 28, 2005

To the Editor:

Your editorial ("Hamas Enters Politics") erroneously posits that Israel's banning of Hamas from the Palestinian parliamentary elections would increase tensions between Israel and the Palestinians. Whether from within or without the Palestinian Authority, Hamas can be relied upon to escalate its assault upon Israel after the elections. Significantly, a Hamas-controlled government would have access not only to the Palestinian treasury – whatever that's worth after Arafat & Co. looted about $1 billion – but to the weaponry and vast armaments.

It needs to be pointed out that a democratically elected legislature is not synonymous with a democratic government. Participation in the political process will not draw Hamas into a democratic model any more than such participation did with Hizbullah's election to the Lebanese government, or the Peronistas in Argentina. Indeed, Hamas has repeatedly stated that its election to the Palestinian National Council would have *no* effect on its determination to destroy Israel. And consider further that the PLO agreed at Oslo that terrorists could not stand for election. Is that to be another Palestinian promise to be relegated to the junk heap?

Finally, conceding that Hamas could win the election, you still urge Israel not to sacrifice "its principles" just to avoid "a new set of dilemmas." The first duty of a nation is to protect its citizens, and Israel simply can't do that if it follows your advice and facilitates the election of a terrorist government which, you acknowledge, would "thwart the peace process" and which is dedicated to her destruction.

For the Record

January 6, 2006

To the Editor (NYT):

Your comment that "the Israelis can't live with the Palestinians" (Editorial: "Life After Sharon" 1/6/06) puts the shoe on the wrong foot. It is the Palestinians who can't live with the Israelis.

There is one undeniable fact that clears away the smoke and illuminates this truth: Israel's disengagement from Gaza was necessary because 1.4 million Palestinians wouldn't live in peace with 8,000 Israelis. That is the reason Gaza, with the encouragement of the United States and Europe, became an apartheid state.

Israel and the Palestinians – What the Media Aren't Telling You

January 17, 2006

To the Editor (NYT):

King Abdullah argues that the alternative to a Palestinian state is chaos. The question really is: What kind of Palestinian state? But I would go further and suggest that the establishment of a Palestinian state under current circumstances is also a formula for chaos.

If the Palestinian parliamentary elections are held on January 25, it seems clear that Hamas will come out with a substantial enough percentage of the vote, if not an outright majority, to see it demand more than just "a seat at the table." This means cabinet posts and sufficient influence in security and diplomatic affairs as to effectively control the Palestinian Authority. This was made possible in large part by the incompetence of President Abbas, who did nothing to democratize the PA and wipe out corruption. The balance of Hamas's appeal to the Palestinian electorate comes largely from Hamas's credible claim for responsibility for Israel's disengagement from Gaza.

Under the circumstances, Israel will have no alternative but to refuse to recognize or negotiate with a Hamas-controlled Palestinian Authority. To the old saw that says "one can only make peace with one's enemies," I add a caveat: unless that enemy is hell-bent on your destruction. Any negotiated peace would be a Trojan Horse; merely another step toward the phased destruction of Israel. Based on Hamas's comments within the past month, there can be no doubt of Hamas's murderous intentions, whether or not it joins the Palestinian Authority.

A little history is in order: Jordan's King Hussein, in July 1988, ceded all jurisdiction and responsibility for the entire West Bank and East Jerusalem to the PLO. The composition of the Jordanian and West Bank populations is largely what makes this possible. After all, Jordan was supposed to be home to the Palestinian Arabs, the Jordanian population being predominantly Palestinian. For 17 years, between 1950, when King Hussein unilaterally annexed the West Bank and East Jerusalem, and 1967, when Israel conquered the West Bank and reunified Jerusalem, the West Bank Arabs – whom we now call "Palestinians" – lived in relative peace with the Jordanians and the Israelis.

King Hussein wanted a confederation of the West and East Banks with autonomy for the West Bank Palestinians, but under Jordanian rule. In fact, in 1985 Hussein agreed to aid the PLO in coordinating a joint peace initiative. Unable to come to terms, Hussein in 1988 washed his hands of the West Bank and East Jerusalem, dissolved the Jordanian parliament, half of whom were West Bank representatives, and stopped paying salaries to over 20,000 West Bank civil servants.

Now it is almost 18 years later. Arafat is dead, and the Israeli government is desirous of separating itself from the Palestinians under conditions guarantying Israel's security. A confederation with Jordan – first advanced by President Reagan – under which the Palestinians would retain some degree of autonomy and meet their national aspirations, would have separated them from the Israelis and reunited them with their 1947 brethren. The Israelis and the Palestinians could then love each other from a distance.

The issue of military security from missiles and rockets was unlikely to be resolved by a boundary. That, however, would become a matter of conventional war, for which gratefully the Israelis have a strong upper hand.

The issues of contiguity with Gaza and the so-called "right of return" were not even serious matters on the table.

In any event, Reagan couldn't pull it off and Hussein was none too anxious to see it succeed. More than two decades later, more blood has been spilled, negotiating positions have hardened and, more important, there is no peace partner for Israel. All things considered, the likelihood of successful negotiations between Israel and the Palestinians has diminished to the size of a quark.

Israel and the Palestinians – What the Media Aren't Telling You

January 24, 2006

To the Editor (WSJ):

The problem with the prospect of Hamas garnering a victory in the Palestinian elections is not, as you say, that the Palestinians will have to live with their decision. Rather, the problem is that the Israelis will have to live with that reality.

You may be correct that the United States will not "endorse the aims of Hamas simply because it was able to win the votes of a desperate population," but some of the Europeans are already lining up to establish diplomatic relations with this band of murderers. Should Hamas be successful, we may also expect to see Kofi Annan standing in line to shake hands with the "new, democratic" Palestinian leadership. The United Nations, with American tax dollars, will then fund so many more outstanding Palestinian hospitals and universities of the caliber that we have long admired in Gaza, Jenin and Ramallah. The Europeans need a healthy dose of realism. Churchill well understood the nature of the beast when he intoned that he would have no parley with Hitler's murderous gang.

Insofar as economic support is concerned, depending on the depths of the economic exigencies, Hamas, if backed against the wall by a civil war, may, however unlikely, make the same credible denunciations of terrorism as issued from Arafat in Oslo or, more likely, sue for a truce. Yet, Hamas will refuse to disarm because Hamas will have become the Palestinian Authority. Its arms will be the arms of the people, and no one will take those away.

Finally, to suggest that "once in power they might even become more responsible" is whistling in the dark. The marriage of terror and democracy bears the fruit of tyranny, not freedom.

For the Record

January 27, 2006

To the Editor (NYT):

Your editorial ("In the Mideast, a Giant Step Back") suggests that with its election to power, perhaps Hamas will renounce its call for the destruction of Israel, disarm its private army, improve life for the Palestinians and try to negotiate the creation of a Palestinian state. It's time to stop fooling ourselves and face the hard reality.

For the record, Hamas has already reaffirmed that it will neither disarm nor alter the opiate it regularly delivers: Palestine *Judenrein* "from the river to the sea." Indeed, Hamas has already admitted that any peace agreement with Israel is merely one step in its staged plan for the destruction of the Jewish state. It is disingenuous of the *Times* to try to explain this away on the ground that the phased destruction of Israel was not prominent in Hamas's campaign literature.

Insofar as the demand from President Bush and the various EU leaders that Hamas renounce terrorism and recognize Israel's right to exist peacefully behind secure borders, I recall this same promise made many times by Arafat. The problems are twofold: First, Arafat's message of peace was in English, but his message in Arabic was to fill the land with the blood of the Jews. We never called him on it. If you want to know what Hamas means, listen to what it tells its people in their language. Second, the Palestinians have never honored their agreements. If Hamas issues a statement – or even signs an agreement – recognizing Israel and renouncing terrorism, I have no doubt that its words will lie rotting in the sewer beside broken Palestinian promises past.

This leopard will not change its spots, because it now has no incentive to do so. The Palestinians overwhelmingly voted for Hamas and, therefore, its *modus vivendi*. They are now the elected representatives of the Palestinians. Democracy in action. Moreover, it has on its side the force of a credible argument that it chased Israel out of Gaza. Its efforts to do so in the West Bank are only a matter of time.

February 1, 2006

To the Editor (JP):

There is a very poignant scene at the end of the 1961 movie *Judgment at Nuremberg* in which the American judge, played by Spencer Tracy, visits the jail cell of a convicted German judge, played by Burt Lancaster. Lancaster pleads with Tracy to believe him that he never thought "it would come to this." Tracy looks at him sadly and says, "Herr Janning, the first time you sentenced a man you knew to be innocent, you knew it would come to this."

Now that Hamas has won control of the Palestinian Authority, there are the usual recriminations, accusations and apportionment of blame. Abbas is to blame for not weeding out corruption and eliminating anarchy. The Palestinians are to blame for letting a culture of death guide their hands over the ballots. Sharon is to blame for not giving Abbas more concessions, as though Gaza were not enough. The United States is to blame for not holding Sharon's feet to the fire, etc., etc.

How did this happen? How did the bad guys win? Almost everyone had a hand in it. Of course Abbas was wrong not to clean out the Augean stables known as the Palestinian Authority. Perhaps it is true that one of the reasons the Palestinians voted for Hamas was the PA's failure to run a clean government. Certainly, armed militias running amok and routinely raiding government offices demanding, and often getting, jobs had something to do with it. From the hundreds of millions of dollars received by the PA, not one refugee camp was demolished and replaced with decent housing. In the absence of a judicial system, there was no legal means to redress grievances. The PA's security forces were comprised of the militias. The give-a-criminal-a-badge-and-a-gun philosophy of law enforcement just didn't cut it. Anarchy was the *plat du jour* and daylight murder was commonplace. And I can't help feeling that overt anti-Semitism played a part in moving the Palestinians into the Hamas fold. Hamas had, in fact, forced the Israelis to retreat from Gaza. Perhaps a Palestine "from the river to the sea" was, in the hands of Hamas, not an impossible dream.

As for Sharon, his unilateral disengagement from Gaza gave Hamas the credibility it needed to claim that terrorism drove the Israelis out. Apply enough pain, and you can make a horse deal cards. In the Middle East, the illusion is often more important than the reality. The minute the Israelis withdrew their army, settlers and, yes, their dead, there was no reason to believe that Gaza would not descend into anarchy and become the Palestinian warehouse for AK-47s, bullets, Kassam rockets, explosives, missiles, incitement and treachery.

As soon as Israel disengaged from Gaza and the Philadelphi Corridor, the American secretary of state was close behind insisting that Israel permit convoys of trucks and buses to pass unmolested from Gaza to the West Bank. It was precisely at that time, however, that the US should have tightened security at the crossings to control anyone and anything going from Gaza to Nablus, Ramallah, Jenin and Jericho. Apparently, it was more important for the United States to appear evenhanded. After all, someone other than the French had to throw a bone to the Palestinians.

As for holding Sharon's feet to the fire to induce further concessions, everything that could have been squeezed out of Israel at that time already had been. Sharon was facing a near mutiny at home. And wasn't it time to demand that the Palestinians do something, anything, to advance the so-called peace process?

Or perhaps the fault lie in letting Hamas participate in the elections. As much as Oslo was appeasement, at least the Israelis secured the Palestinian agreement that no terrorist group could participate in elections. This was sound policy, which the Israelis had in fact imposed on themselves. (Israel had years earlier banned the late Meir Kahane's Kach Party, which advocated the expulsion of all Arabs from Israel.) Why did Israel relent on that important issue? Was it because Abbas threatened not to hold the elections without Hamas? Was it because the Americans persuaded the Israelis that in a democracy everyone must have the right to run for elective office, or, perhaps because we thought that an election without a popular party lacked legitimacy? Whatever the reason,

Hamas walked into the Palestinian legislature because someone opened the door for them. Anyone who did not see this coming was either not looking or fast asleep.

So how did this happen? Perhaps it was Abbas succumbing to political inertia. Perhaps it was Sharon letting the Palestinians have Gaza without a *quid pro quo*. Perhaps it was the US not holding Abbas's feet to the fire to get the Palestinians moving. Or perhaps it was as simple as letting the Palestinians off the hook by letting Hamas on the ballot. Whether it was any one or a combination of all these missteps, it is clear that as matters stood last week, the election of Hamas was inevitable. Under the circumstances, as Spencer Tracy might have said, it had already come to that.

For the Record

February 27, 2006

To the Editor (JP):

In "Livni Says Abbas a Powerless Leader," it is pointed out that the United States and European Union have suggested they will keep working with "moderate" Palestinian President Abbas even if a Hamas government takes office in the coming weeks. To this end, EU foreign ministers were expected to approve continued aid to the Palestinian caretaker government. That could include paying $48 million to help run utilities and authorizing the World Bank to unblock $60 million to pay Palestinian salaries. Thus another $108 million will find its way into the treasury of the Hamas government. It goes without saying that this flies in the face of everything the US and the EU had threatened about withholding financial aid since Hamas's velvet *coup d'etat*. This would be bad enough by itself, but the avowed purpose of the emergency funding is to prop up President Abbas.

This excuse for sending money to the Palestinians will fail on two counts. First and foremost, nothing can save Abbas from irrelevance and impotence. The Palestinian people have spoken and Fatah has fallen with a resounding thud. Second, Abbas is not worth saving. With all the time and money the international community had thrown at him, Abbas refused to do even one thing to bring the parties closer to ending the conflict. Indeed, it could well be argued that matters are now worse than when he took office. Whether this was the result of incompetence or malice is now beside the point.

The Palestinian people have cast their lot with Hamas. Let them have what they have called for in such a strong voice. And let America and the rest of the Quartet withhold the aid they have foresworn. We should not try to save the Palestinians from themselves when they, in a collective voice, demand another Holocaust.

When Israel declared her independence almost 58 years ago, the world stood by as the Arabs tried to complete Hitler's final solution and annihilate an infant democracy. It was reasoned that if Israel were to survive in a hostile world it had better be able to survive that early war. The same thing should be said of the Hamas government. And it's time for America and the Europeans to stand by their principles and to stop worrying whether the Arabs will still love us.

For the Record

March 13, 2006

To the Editor (Newsday):

The cement has barely dried and already there are serious cracks in the wall between Western money and the Hamas government. I'm not talking about Iran or the other Arab states. I'm referring to Russia, France, what's left of the Quartet, the United Nations, the EU and the World Bank. Once Hamas was elected, all of these states and organizations declared from atop a feeble moral foundation built on feigned courage that they would not deal with terrorists or a terrorist government. No sooner were the principles enunciated than exceptions proliferated.

First, President Putin cut the Quartet loose and announced that the Russians would meet with Hamas's top leaders. (This, remarkably enough, after Chechan terrorists in September 2004 caused the deaths of 344 civilians, including 186 schoolchildren.) Then the French sniffed their approval. Soon, you didn't have enough fingers and toes to count all the countries that had gone from "never" to "let's see what Hamas becomes when they form a government." After every meeting in Europe and Arabia, Hamas reiterated its dedication to the destruction of Israel "from the river to the sea." Nevertheless, mountains of money poured in to keep the PA solvent and capable of meeting its payroll, and thus avoid the presumed consequence of economic meltdown followed by complete anarchy.

It became more important to keep Hamas afloat – as if it were going to morph into a bicameral republic – than to see if it had the ability to govern. This nonsensical chatter from the cheap seats gives the 21st century its first real example of appeasement. Hamas is radical Islam and one would have thought by now that lesson had been learned by the Danes, British, French, Russians and Spanish. What is it about radical Islam that compels us to give it moral authority? Why is a Hamas-run government worthy of sustenance?

Second, the prickly issue of humanitarian assistance. America's resident supplicant, former President Jimmy Carter, offered that if the Palestinians suffer they will become angry and hate the United States. Mr. Carter raises an interesting equation: The more we are hated, the more generous we should be to those who would kill us. Mr. Carter's thinking, such as it is, does not have anything to do with humanitarianism, but rather politics, in this case his whining obsession with unrequited love of America.

The problem with humanitarian aid is that money is fungible. Unless we are capable of tracing the actual disbursement of monies, follow what they pay for, and then observe how and where those products are administered, then the exercise is meaningless. I thought we had learned as much from Saddam Hussein, who sold humanitarian goods to buy arms. What must be understood is that even humanitarian aid to the Palestinians has the effect of freeing up money for terrorism.

Which brings us to the questions of accountability and consequences. Should the Palestinian people be made to suffer for the acts of Hamas? It is clear that, by an overwhelming majority, the Palestinians elected Hamas and discarded Fatah. It is also clear that everyone knew who and what Hamas was and stood for. Hamas's foreign policy is straightforward and unconditional: to destroy Israel and to make all of Palestine *Judenrein*, just as they accomplished, with American and European support, in Gaza.

Unless one is prepared to say that they were bamboozled, the Palestinians got exactly what they wanted: a homicidal, irredentist regime that pushed Israel out of Gaza and which promises to do the same in all of Judea, Samaria and the rest of Israel. And this is what makes the "humanitarian" issue a canard: You cannot separate the Palestinians from Hamas. It is futile to try to distinguish between the electorate and the freely elected. What's more, it is wrong to do so. The Palestinians should not be relieved of the consequences of what they did and who they declared resoundingly to be their representatives. So far no one has advanced a cogent or persuasive reason to give aid and comfort to the enemy. And by "enemy" I don't refer only to Hamas. I include the Palestinian people. They chose Hamas and its bloody path. It is the Palestinian people that must be held accountable for their choice. And in case no one noticed, since Hamas's election and foreign warnings to cut off funds, the Palestinians have stood behind their choice. Indeed, the Palestinians sneer at American threats.

If we continue to bail out the Palestinians we will be taken for fools – and rightly so. (The Iranians with their project for "peaceful" nuclear power laugh as they recount how they lied to the rest of the world for the past 20+ years.) No sooner did the Western powers declare that a Hamas-led Palestinian government must be quarantined than a line has formed to give them hundreds of millions of dollars. It is difficult to believe that their sole motivation for doing so is humanitarian.

I can think of no rationale for saving the Palestinian Authority from withering on the vine. If Hamas does succeed, it will not be from having been planted in the fertile soil of democracy, but rather from being nurtured in the stuff of treachery.

Israel and the Palestinians – What the Media Aren't Telling You

March 16, 2006

To the Editor (NYT):

Your lead editorial ("As if That Fire Needed Fuel,") casting Israel in the role of predator for capturing the murderers of its cabinet minister Rehavam Ze'evi stands reason on its head. Rather than reprehension, Israel should be applauded for restoring, even if for only one day, the democratic rule of law in Jericho, a city no sane man would enter without benefit of a tank and body armor.

Seemingly lost in this debate is who the Palestinians murdered. Ze'evi was the minister of tourism, a member of the Israeli cabinet. Israel cannot stand by when one of its cabinet ministers is murdered in cold blood. For Israel to have permitted the Palestinian gangsters to get away would have been a violation of every civilized nation's obligation to protect its citizens and to enforce the rule of law on those who violate it.

The suggestion that "Hamas should not have provoked Israel with chatter about freeing Saadat" is disingenuous. Hamas represents the Palestinian government and characterizing its promise to release Saadat and Co. as mere "chatter" trivializes how real the threat actually was. Making the threat that much more real was President Abbas's complicity.

Curiously, you condemn Israel for having had the Palestinian inmates strip to their underwear. You use strong words: "embarrassing and completely unnecessary," a "provocation," "trampled the dignity," "humiliation," and last, but not least, "the already degrading reality of living under foreign occupation." It is apparently necessary to remind you who these "people" are: murderers of a cabinet minister of the Middle East's only democracy and America's only true ally. Given the porous security at the Jericho prison, the Israelis took the reasonable measure of ascertaining whether the prisoners were carrying or concealing weapons or explosives. Protecting one's military is another right you would deny Israel.

I note the response of Mr. Abbas, who was whining and dining in Europe at the time. Upon his return to Jericho, the impotent

Palestinian president called the raid "an unforgivable crime and an insult to the Palestinian people." Mr. Abbas had it backwards. The unforgivable crime was the murder of an Israeli minister. The insults were that Saadat, a murderer, was elected to the Palestinian National Council from jail, that the killers lived a country club life, and were soon going to be released by Hamas. In fact, with the loss of the British and American monitors – owing to the PA's refusal to provide adequate security for them – it is entirely likely that had the IDF not then appeared, the Palestinians would have immediately swept the six murderers to a safe harbor from which they could have been extricated only at the end of a long and bloody battle. That the Palestinian guards at the Jericho prison engaged the Israelis in combat is sufficient proof of their complicity.

Why should Israel let the murderers of a cabinet minister walk away from that crime? To do so would be tantamount to relinquishing its right of self-defense, for this too was very much an attack on the Israeli nation, its ministers being, so to speak, the embodiment of the state.

Over the months since Israel withdrew from Gaza, the Palestinians have daily tested the Israelis with rocket fire, attempts to kidnap IDF soldiers, smuggling of arms and ammunition and suicide-bombers. The Israeli response has been, at best, weak. Many believe Israel has lost her deterrent credibility. There has been no *quid pro quo* for Palestinian terrorism, which has the disastrous effect of emboldening the terrorists. This swift and forceful military operation was vitally important to remind the Palestinians what they should expect from Israel in the future and to give them a small taste to remind them of the IDF's capabilities.

Although you also criticize Israel for taking this action so close to elections, perhaps that is also what this should be about: the knowledge that Israel can and will respond forcefully to crimes against her government and citizens. Whatever Olmert's motivation, this salutary act was necessary and appropriate. And whatever else may be said, these were Palestinian crimes that necessitated Israeli action, not the other way around as Abbas, Mashaal, Erekat & Co. now aver.

Finally, to take the position urged by the *Times* that it was wrong to apprehend the Palestinians by necessity argues that Israel should have done nothing, and watched the men who murdered Ze'evi disappear into the night, escaping accountability and justice, free to exercise their homicidal franchise.

For the Record

March 23, 2006

To the Editor (NYT):

Gideon Lichfield's Op-Ed ("Cuba on the West Bank") falls short on several points. First on foreign policy grounds. Whereas Castro has no intention, much less the capability, to destroy the United States, the obliteration of Israel is Hamas's *raison d'être*, proven in both word and deed. Castro may rant and rave, but Hamas has successfully sent suicide-bombers to kill and terrorize Israelis for more than five years. Unfortunately, it is only likely to get worse as Hamas allies itself with Iran and Syria.

His point that 75% of Palestinians support peace talks with Israel, if true, must be tempered by the knowledge that these same Palestinians gave Hamas a resounding electoral victory two months ago and rings hollow against the daily pronouncements of Hamas's leaders demanding Israel's destruction. The Palestinians knew this when they voted for Hamas. Moreover, the basis on which Hamas is willing to start talks is *after* Israel has withdrawn to the "Auschwitz borders." A non-starter if ever there was one.

The social-economic situation in Cuba and Gaza lie in stark contrast. As Mr. Lichfield notes, because of substantial European investment in industry and tourism the Cubans aren't dying in the streets. Gaza, on the other hand, is not exactly beating investors away. No one will bring capital to the Palestinian economy, because people walk the streets of Gaza in fear and know that sooner or later Hamas is going to take the fight back to Israel, as it has promised. Can you imagine the Ritz Carlton opening a $50 million hotel and health spa on the beautiful Mediterranean Sea only blocks from Gaza City's central business district? As my brother says, "Not even on the moon."

The argument that a capitalized Palestinian Authority will bring social stability is also unsupportable, as we've witnessed in the past two months. Indeed, even if Hamas were successful in ending Palestinian anarchy, for which it acknowledges it has no plans, we'd still be left with a Hamastan devoted to destroying

Israel. That being the case, it is also irrelevant whether Abbas holds the "one gun."

Israel is fighting for her life, and Mr. Lichfield's plan to deal with Israel using a "carrot and stick" policy sadly attributes moral equivalence to a democratic Israel and a terrorist Palestinian Authority. And lest it be overlooked, the Cubans love life and their children, whereas the Palestinians are eager to sacrifice both for the privilege of killing a Jew. Cuba on the West Bank? Israel should be so lucky.

For the Record

March 30, 2006

To the Editor (NYT):

Your editorial "West Bank Withdrawal" (3/30/06) misses the mark because it takes only the short view, and a distorted one at that. This conflict is existential; it is not a border dispute.

Stating that "the ultimate solution to the conflict can be only a negotiated one," is disingenuous. The Palestinians elected a regime dedicated to Israel's destruction; Hamas named a cabinet composed entirely of implacable extremists. Yet, you relentlessly blame Israel for a "self-created problem." Is it meaningless that the Palestinians have violated every agreement they have made? Is it irrelevant that since Hamas's velvet *coup d'état*, the number of terrorist incidents has increased and that now, for the first time, Katyusha rockets are fired from Gaza? Do you draw succor from Hamas's position that it will recognize past agreements only to the extent it serves their treacherous intent?

Israel is facing an irrational, murderous foe which sees itself as the instrument of extreme Islam. There is no one with whom to negotiate. One need only read the Hamas covenant to realize this. Listen to their proclamation: The highest honor is to die in *jihad* against the Zionists for every inch of Palestine from the river to the sea.

Between 66–73 CE, the Romans starved and then massacred almost the entire Jewish population of Judea, looted and burned the Second Temple, and destroyed the great city of Jerusalem. Some 600,000 Jews died. Bodies by the thousands were left rotting in the streets. There was nothing left. The seat of Rabbinic leadership had to be transferred from Jerusalem to Yavne. That's what this "conflict" is about.

April 7, 2006

To the Editor (NYT):

Your article "US Redirects Aid to Palestinians" reveals the painful choices we face when confronting the dichotomy between a rogue government one wishes to damage, and its citizens, who voted them in but whom one does not seek to harm. The Palestinians present us with a substantive variation on that theme.

Trying to "redirect" American aid away from Hamas and to the people requires one to ignore the seminal fact that the Hamas government came to office in free, democratic elections. It was a choice the Palestinians freely arrived at, with full knowledge of Hamas's agenda.

Humanitarian aid is not so simple to define or administer. Money is fungible and every dollar the West beneficently pumps into the health system, for example, frees up a dollar for the manufacture of Kassam rockets, which is going on at breakneck speed in Gaza. And why should we fund an educational system which daily preaches hatred of and death to the United States?

We are told that the purpose of withholding all but humanitarian aid is to punish Hamas, but not the Palestinians. Yet I am unpersuaded that the Palestinian people should not be held responsible for what it has freely chosen. Why should the concepts of free choice and accountability be divorced for the benefit of a people that urge death and global Islamic domination?

These are people who would not hesitate, if they could, to destroy America and Europe. It is not fear, respect or the value of human life which stops the Palestinians from vaporizing us. Only that they lack the capability.

For the Record

May 4, 2006

To the Editor (JP):

The news that Prime Minister-elect Olmert plans to meet with PLO Chairman Abbas comes as little surprise, particularly when one considers that the announcement came from his primary handler, Shimon Peres. ("Peres to Post: Olmert to Meet Abbas").

If such a meeting is an attempt to do an end run around Hamas or prop up the impotent chairman, it is destined to failure. However, it is also possible that the purpose of such a meeting is to provide the appearance of an attempt to negotiate with the Palestinians. Of course Mr. Abbas would like to make it look like he is the head of government in much the same way as my ex-mother-in-law thought she looked like Grace Kelly. Olmert will insist that Abbas disarm the terrorists, Abbas will say he can't do it, and Olmert will declare that in the absence of a genuine negotiating partner with real authority, Israel must proceed unilaterally.

The real loose cannon in your report is Vice Premier Shimon Peres. Israel's appeaser nonpareil continues to smile even when facing the barrel of a gun. His pronouncements, if uttered by a civilian, would be dismissed as lunacy. But coming from a high-ranking member of the Israeli government, they are nothing short of frightening. Frankly, his presence in the government unnerves me.

Mr. Peres – notwithstanding daily declarations by Hamas of its murderous intent, the Palestinians' recent use of the advanced Katyusha rockets and the significant increase in bombing attempts, thankfully prevented by the IDF – stressed that any agreement would have to be made with Abbas, rather than Hamas. This in spite of the fact that Abbas couldn't organize a turkey shoot. After all, Mr. Peres opines, Mr. Abbas is "an honorable man. He means peace."

The bill of particulars of Mr. Abbas's failures is the length of your arm. Before Hamas came to office, Abbas made absolutely no effort to comply with any Palestinian obligation under the Road Map. For example, he didn't lift a finger to disarm the terrorists or root out corruption within his own government. He refused to halt the anti-Israel and anti-Semitic indoctrination of schoolchildren. He was unable to stabilize the situation in Gaza; in fact, he presided over its descent into anarchy. And he left the Palestinian Authority on the edge of bankruptcy. This is a man of "peace" and "honor"?

The principal problem, which Peres fails to grasp, is that Abbas is merely Hamas in a suit. His methods vary, but his objective is the same. But even if Abbas were the real thing, he still lacks the support of the Palestinian people, the majority of whom in a recent poll declare that Hamas should not recognize Israel, support armed attacks against Israeli civilians, and two-thirds of whom said they believe that armed confrontation accomplishes more than negotiation.

On the explosive issue of Iran, Mr. Peres is quoted as saying that Iran "is a world problem and I think the world has to handle it," adding that Israel should let the US and other responsible partners take the lead when it comes to a nuclear threat from Iran. The ability to distinguish between reality and wishful thinking seems to have eluded him, and his comment that "We are not an enemy of Iran," is the utterance of an unsound mind unsuitable to acting in a governmental capacity.

These are precarious times: Hamas proudly repeats, as if hatred were a virtue, that Israel must be destroyed and all its Jews killed, deported or converted to Islam. Gaza has descended into chaos and the only thing preventing the West Bank from following suit is the presence of the IDF. Rival Palestinian terrorist groups, various clans and "committees" are killing each other. Terrorism is on the rise and the Hamas government aids, abets and encourages it, refusing to take any action against those who commit it. Al-Qaida has established footholds in Gaza and the West Bank, and Hamas is cozying up to Russia, Syria and, worse yet, Iran.

All the while, Mr. Peres practices appeasement and declares that Iran is not a threat to Israel. The substantive danger to Israel, at this moment, is that Shimon Peres, the vice premier of Israel, is unable to distinguish between spit and rain.

May 16, 2006

To the Editor (JP):

Barry Rubin's article ("Why Bail Hamas Out?" May 16, 2006) correctly points out the lunacy of funding the Palestinian Authority for all but health and sanitation services. But I would like to suggest another salient reason to withhold other funds: We would be rewarding the Palestinians for turning their government over to terrorists.

Just before the Palestinian legislative elections of this past January, the United States and the EU all threatened sanctions and the withholding of economic aid to a Hamas-run Palestinian Authority. We were firm and resolute that no democracy would fund a terrorist government. We would, so to speak, stop Hitler at Munich.

The Palestinians took up the challenge and gave Hamas a landslide victory. Terrorism, not negotiations led by Abu Mazen, drove the Israelis out of Gaza. Hamas led the fight; Fatah was too busy looting the treasury.

Threats to cut the Palestinians loose if they elected Hamas meant nothing. The Palestinians and Hamas announced that they needed neither American charity nor European largesse. Israel withheld the $50 million a month in taxes it had collected for the Palestinian Authority. The World Bank was going to hold back its money, the Americans and Europeans theirs.

The Palestinians themselves stood shoulder to shoulder with the terrorists they elected to lead their government. Angry and defiant, Hamas told the Quartet to go to hell.

For two months now, government salaries, which feed one-third of the population in Gaza, have not been paid. They said they would get the money from their Arab brethren – $50 million from Iran, another couple of million here, another million there. It wasn't enough to meet even one month's payroll. Still, the Palestinians tell us to go to hell. Recently, the Palestinians in Gaza and the West Bank lined up to sell their gold and family jewelry.

Anything to put some money in their pockets. "Go ahead," they taunt us, "We don't care. There is nothing you can do to us."

The singular weakness of Sharon's decision to remove the Jews of Gaza was that it was unilateral and complete. No *quid pro quo*. Israel received *nothing* in return. "We give up. We can't take it. We're leaving." The consequences on the ground were the planting of al-Qaida cells in Gaza and permitting Gaza to grow into the world's largest open-air arms factory and market, as well as a stopping-off point for terrorists to rearm on the way to Judea and Samaria. Significantly, the unilateral withdrawal by its very nature created a vacuum which the jihadists naturally filled.

The greatest triumph for the Palestinians was the very real perception that Israel had been driven out of Gaza by terrorism, that terrorism works against a democracy. Kids throwing rocks and firebombs, blowing themselves and Israeli civilians to bits, and a resistance armed with nothing more than hatred, the desire to die and some guns and dynamite defeated the greatest military power ever known in the Middle East. Disengagement gave the Palestinians not merely a military victory over Israel, it gave them momentum and the encouragement to escalate matters.

The fact that an all-out assault by the IDF and the IAF would have leveled Gaza in fewer than six days was irrelevant because it was not an option. Sharon and Peres did not want to do that. So, instead of letting the Palestinians know what they were up against, Israel withdrew with a whimper. And the Palestinians celebrated and continue to lob Kassam rockets from Gaza into Israel.

And now it's happening again. This week, the Quartet – or what's left of it after the Russians broke ranks and met with Hamas officials – announced a plan to set up a trust fund that would possibly pay salaries of health and education workers, which comprise a quarter of the PA's workforce of about 165,000 people. Forget for now what it would mean to pay the salaries of the Palestinian teachers who daily inculcate anti-Americanism and anti-Semitism, among other hatreds, into young minds. The fact is that our money will support a government which makes no bones about its fiery desire to kill us all. We are handing the Palestinians another freebie, another gift on a silver platter in exchange for which they must do…nothing.

More than just relinquishing the high moral ground, we are now ready to give the Palestinians another *gratis* victory. They are going to get money without accepting Israel's right to exist. They are going to get money without accepting a two-state solution. They are going to get money without accepting any past PA/PLO agreements with Israel. They are going to get money while they continue to kill Israelis; while they increase the number of suicide-bombers sent into Israel's cafes and while they continue, without meaningful consequence, to shell Israeli cities with Kassams and Katyusha rockets. More momentum.

And once again, the unworthy Palestinians will take our money and spit in our faces. Why is it that we are not resolute enough to stand up to this Neanderthal culture? Do we not understand that betraying our first principles gives the Palestinian people another victory, another reward for murder, recidivism, obdurate intolerance and hate? What do we think will come of that?

In the play *The Fantastiks*, two fathers bemoan what their son and daughter have become. "Plant a radish, you get a radish," one tells the other. If we continue to reward hatred, it should come as no surprise when it is hatred that grows. Or, as the Bible says, as ye sow, so shall ye reap.

For the Record

May 18, 2006

To the Editor (NYT):

Re: "Iran Snubs Europe's Nuclear Plan," (May 18). Every time I read how Europe is reacting to the Iranian crisis I shake my head in disbelief. The newest European plan had not even been presented when Iran rejected it out of hand. True to form, the Europeans delayed the presentation to sweeten the offer. Why is such consequential policy being written by people who are so seemingly ignorant of Ahmadinejad's character and intentions?

Iran's intentions being clear, instead of appeasing it, we should be instituting immediately economic and financial sanctions. For example, Iran is on our terror list. Just as we did with Hamas, America should make it known that every bank involved in Iranian fiscal affairs will be criminally prosecuted. Iran imports 40% of its gasoline. Enforce an embargo.

Those are just two actions we can take to get the mullahs' attention without engaging military forces, an option which we should make clear is always on the table.

This is not the time for diplomacy. Proposals to sweeten the deal only make the Iranians laugh at us. It's time for Europe to walk away from the table. We need to take proactive steps to incentivize Iran's Hitler-wannabe.

Israel and the Palestinians – What the Media Aren't Telling You

May 25, 2006

To the Editor (NYT):

Your editorial demand ("A Viable Palestinian State") that Israeli Prime Minister Olmert do nothing without bilateral negotiations is flawed on several levels, the first being your suggestion that the Palestinians are not responsible for the murderous intent of their democratically elected government. The contrary is true. The Palestinian Authority is indeed a representative government.

It is disingenuous to charge Israel with damaging the prospects of peace because she will not negotiate with people who insist on her death. Tell us then: with whom should Israel negotiate? It is, in fact, the Palestinians who destroy the prospects for peace by continuing to kill Israelis. Olmert is charged with defending his people, not playing nursemaid to the Palestinians.

You argue that convergence is bad because it ignores the Palestinians' rights. No, it is wrong because it ignores both what Judea and Samaria will become under their jurisdiction – another Gaza – and the character and ambitions of the Palestinians.

For the Record

June 2, 2006

To the Editor (Newsday):

Last night before I went to bed, I went into my daughters' rooms and, as is my daily custom, kissed them each on the forehead. "Good night, cookie. I love you," I would whisper so as not to awaken them.

Something happened in Israel yesterday that reminded me of my little ritual. A short story in *The Jerusalem Post*, it was apparently not significant enough to be picked up by the American newspapers or news services. Yet, it was a Palestinian statement having no less import than their choice that Hamas should rule over them.

It should first be noted that the Gaza security fence has become the scene of almost daily attempts at infiltration and terror attacks, and occasionally even exchanges of fire.

A group of four Palestinian children, around thirteen years of age, were sent towards the Gaza Strip border fence holding toy guns. When the children were about 400 meters from the fence, IDF soldiers ascertained that the four were just children and that their weapons were just toys.

There can be little doubt that the Palestinians sent their children on this "mission" in order to provoke the IDF into killing four unarmed children. That the IDF patiently held its fire is not surprising to me. Sadly, neither is the fact that the Palestinians were willing to sacrifice their children for the sole purpose of demonizing the Israelis. No incident could more clearly define the differing values of life to the Israelis and the Palestinians.

I know of no higher-order animal that lacks the instinct to protect its young. Dogs, monkeys, lions and elephants do. Even the lowly bird attacks those who would bring harm to its offspring. Yet the Palestinian, alone among God's creations, sees in his children nothing more than the scandalous means to harm and shame the Israelis. To us, our children are precious, to be loved and nurtured. To the Palestinians, their children are bait.

Israel and the Palestinians – What the Media Aren't Telling You

June 22, 2006

To the Editor (IJP):

The statements of Prime Minister Olmert that he plans to abandon Shilo, Beit El, Ofra and Kedumim, and likely other settlements historically a part of Eretz Yisrael, brings to mind Churchill's remarks when British PM Chamberlain returned from Munich in 1938: "Instead of snatching the victuals from the table, [Hitler] has been content to have them served to him course by course."

Olmert's greatest failing is his belief that relinquishing Judea and Samaria will satisfy the Palestinians, end this conflict and enable the Israelis to live "in partnership" beside a contiguous Palestinian state. Olmert foolishly believes that this is merely a border dispute when in fact it is quite literally existential.

His suggestion that the Jews of Judea and Samaria will have a choice to remain there under Palestinian rule ignores everything that has transpired in the last year. The unilateral retreat from Gaza proved at least two points: First, that the Palestinians will not permit any Jews to live there. Those who remain risk their lives. Second, Israeli withdrawal is a resolute defeat and a mere prelude to chaos and a heavily armed terrorist state.

It is inexplicable that Olmert has already given up on Shilo, et al. The message to the Palestinians is that Hamas, in exchange for nothing, will get them what they want. And therein lies the slim, slender reed upon which Olmert's political philosophy rests: the discredited theory of "land for peace" to which he naively clings. But with these further concessions, Olmert adds a twist: land without peace.

Olmert is fooling himself and misleading the country when he says that the majority of Israelis favors "painful compromises that would put an end to the conflict." Olmert seems unable to grasp that painful concessions will *not* put an end to the conflict. In the Middle East, terrorism always trumps appeasement and weakness, a lesson the Palestinians learned well from Gaza.

Just as Olmert was wrong to think that abandoning Gaza would create stability, he is wrong to believe that unilaterally yielding Judea and Samaria to the Palestinians will be the end of the conflict. The contrary is, in fact, the case. Should he do so, he will have endorsed the election of Hamas and destroyed any chance, however remote, of a peaceful resolution.

Hitler promised that Czechoslovakia was his last territorial demand. One must ask what else Prime Minister Olmert will give the Palestinians in his futile quest to be left alone. We must be mindful of what Churchill also said in 1938: "Mr. Chamberlain's government was given to choose between war and shame. It has chosen shame. It will surely have war."

Israel and the Palestinians – What the Media Aren't Telling You

June 30, 2006

To the Editor (IJP):

Israel's incursion into Gaza comes as a welcome contrast to the government's casual reaction to, among other things, the incessant firing of rockets from Gaza into "pre-1967" Israel. Since the disengagement from Gaza, there has been little evidence that the government understood that it is at war with the Palestinians and not merely bogged down in negotiations. The attitude of the Olmert government seems to have been that as long as no one died, no harm was done. Nothing could have been further from the truth.

To the contrary, it has been Israel's lack of a response to the shelling of Sderot and Ashkelon that has emboldened the Palestinians to believe that they could get away with these murders and kidnapping. By failing to respond to relentless aggression, the Olmert government invited the Palestinians to press the assault and, as could be expected, escalate matters. A seemingly emasculated IDF was apparently ordered to stand by and watch helplessly as Israelis were terrorized by daily rocket fire.

Complement that with last year's unilateral withdrawal from Gaza and Prime Minister Olmert's declaration of his intention to unilaterally withdraw from Judea and Samaria. What could be expected of the Palestinians other than confidence that terrorism works? The deterrent value of the IDF was seemingly illusory.

Israel's rapid response – particularly the arrest of most of the Palestinian government and cabinet – has been the first sign of intelligent life in Jerusalem in several years. As Churchill noted after Dunkirk, wars are not won by evacuations.

The Palestinian attack stunned the government and should have shattered for all time the illusions that Mahmoud Abbas was a peace partner, and that Hamas was a creature with which Israel could do business. When Hamas declared that its *raison d'être* is the extermination of Israel, there was no reason not to take them at their word. And when the Palestinians overwhelmingly cast their lot with Hamas, there was no reason to believe their decision was made with other than open eyes. Instead, Kadima and Labor engaged in the self-delusion that Hamas would reform itself and that the Palestinian vote really meant that they just wanted an end to Fatah corruption and peace with Israel.

What all of this points to is that the disengagement from Gaza was ill-conceived. The Sharon-Olmert-Peres triumvirate assumed, with no evidence, that the Palestinians would be happy with Gaza and build up its economy, thus stabilizing the region. In fact, since the disengagement 10 months ago, more armaments have flowed into Gaza than in the prior 39 years. The Palestinians are not creatures of diplomacy. They are, rather, creatures of war. Again, Israel placed her security in the hands of those who would kill her.

Hamas wants to destroy Israel and the Palestinians are only too eager to help Hamas accomplish their goal. It has always been just that simple. What part of that does the Kadima-Labor government not understand?

July 14, 2006

To the Editor (NYT):

Thomas Friedman is right that the Middle East is entering a dangerous time, but it's not because of the election of terrorists or the hijacking of democracy.

The danger is that Hizbullah has weapons well beyond the 12-kilometer range and the sophistication of the Kassam rockets being fired from Gaza. As we saw yesterday, Haifa is now within Hizbullah's reach, and this gives the terrorists capabilities of an entirely more dangerous dimension. Specifically, what this means is that we are no longer dealing with small villages and towns. Two million Israelis living in the North are now at risk. .

Moreover, if that technology is transferred to the Palestinians in the West Bank and to other terrorists, that would place virtually all major Israeli cities within Palestinian striking distance. And that would represent a sea change in the balance of power, because Israel will no longer be engaged in local skirmishes involving suicide-bombers, but transnational aggression in which hundreds of lives may be wiped out in a single act.

Finally, it must be noted that Israel's use of force in Lebanon is directed at the Lebanese military machinery, while Hizbullah is specifically targeting civilians.

July 17, 2006

To the Editor (IJP):

The precipitous entry of Hizbullah into the Israeli-Palestinian conflict comes at a particularly dangerous time and under circumstances that can only be described as menacing as well as capricious.

Hizbullah leader Nasrallah's decision to invade Israel's northern border, which he acknowledges had nothing to do with Israel's incursion into the Gaza Strip, is intended to do more than provoke. It is a test of Olmert's backbone and Israel's national will. Having watched the Palestinians fire rockets daily from Gaza into pre-1967 Israel for 11 months without consequence, and the IDF now going cautiously into Gaza, this was a propitious time to engage Israel on a second front.

Hizbullah's bombing of Haifa drastically raised the stakes. With the international community waiting to hang Israel for the Lebanese incursion, Israel is warned to act proportionately and to be mindful of civilians. But with Hizbullah and its weaponry hiding in schools, hospitals, houses and apartment buildings, that may be too tall an order. Unless the Lebanese government steps up to the plate and forcibly removes Hizbullah from those sanctuaries, civilian casualties are unavoidable. Given Hizbullah's military strength and popularity, the Lebanese government, such as it is, is no match for Hizbullah, a well-equipped, trained and financed battlefield proxy of Syria and Iran.

You will note that the Palestinians to a man support the kidnappings and murders by both Hamas and Hizbullah. Palestinians were dancing in the street, firing weapons in the air and handing out candy when Hamas struck three weeks ago. The scene repeated itself with greater vigor when Hizbullah struck last week. The Palestinians are giddy over Hamas's and Hizbullah's successes. To the Palestinian man in the street, it doesn't matter how Israel reacts; they have bloodied Israel's nose. They already have their victory and whatever happens in the future they will continue to hate Israel and bow before their terrorist gods, who keep alive their dream of wiping Israel off the map. It is now clear that Israel must reestablish the IDF's superior deterrent capability.

At last count, there were 1,000 rockets and mortars fired into Israel. With the exception of France, no other country would stand around with its hands in its pockets while its citizens are attacked from across an international border. But this being Israel, whose very existence is perpetually questioned, it is again necessary to recreate the wheel and assert her right of self-defense. The only peace Israel can look forward to will be the cease-fire demanded by the UN after, but hopefully not before, Israel has decapitated Hizbullah and destroyed its infrastructure.

To borrow an old physics theorum, three objects cannot occupy the same space at the same time. Those three objects are the Israelis, Hamas and Fatah. And the "space" is Israel.

For the Record

July 17, 2006

Mr. Bob Schieffer,
CBS Evening News
Re: *The Middle East*

Dear Mr. Schieffer:

…What causes me to write is your story about the frog and the scorpion with the punch line "this is the Middle East." I heard it with a different ending which I would like to share with you. When the frog asks the scorpion why it would do something that will kill both of them, the scorpion replies: "You knew I'm a scorpion." In other words, that's what scorpions do; they kill.

By stating that "This is the Middle East" you make no moral distinction between the frog and the scorpion. There is no evil intent, each one doing merely what nature intended. It is the nature of terrorists to cause death. Hamas and Hizbullah don't care if Palestinian or Lebanese civilians die – in fact more is better since it tarnishes Israel's image. When the IDF causes a civilian death, it is not intentional. When Hamas and Hizbullah cause the deaths of Israeli civilians, they have accomplished their immediate goal. Because that's what terrorist do. They kill. Maliciously and indiscriminately.

Israel and the Palestinians – What the Media Aren't Telling You

July 20, 2006

To the Editor (NYT):

Tom Miller's letter requires a short reply. Contrary to Mr. Miller's assertion, the attacks from Lebanon had nothing to do with Israel's incursion into Gaza. That from Hizbullah chief Nasrallah.

Second, it is not "Israel's refusal to honor the result of democratic elections" that is at the root of the conflict with the Palestinians. If that were the case, how does Mr. Miller explain all the terrorism of the last eight decades that predates the elections only six months ago? The reason Israel refuses to "honor" the Palestinian elections is that Hamas is a gang of murderers who declare, as if a virtue, their intention to destroy Israel.

Finally, a democratic election is not indicative of a democracy. A short glimpse into Gaza would reveal that much.

For the Record

July 24, 2006

To the Editor (JP):

Albert Einstein is reputed to have remarked that stupidity consists of repeating the same experiment under identical conditions, and expecting a different result. In that vein, the recent comments of Lebanese Prime Minister Siniora leap to mind. Reiterating Palestinian President Abbas's plan to deal with Hamas, Siniora stated that once Hizbullah is disarmed – he doesn't say how or by whom – "our government will be able to say that Hizbullah has no legitimate reason to maintain an armed militia. It will inevitably be forced to become a purely political force in our democratic system."

In case the Lebanese prime minister has been asleep for the past six years, Hizbullah has indeed become part of its democratic system, Israel has completely withdrawn from Lebanon, Hizbullah has established itself as the dominant political and military force within Lebanon's borders, and Hizbullah has provoked a war with Israel by crossing an international border and murdering eight Israeli soldiers and kidnapping two others.

The suggestion that a disarmed Hizbullah will turn to the ways of democracy ignores the character, goals and popular support of these murderers; the experience with Hamas, for example, teaches us otherwise. It is a terrorist organization and it is armed to the teeth. Its fanatic hatred for Israel is incapable of behavior modification. If these Muslim extremists are so anxious to get to heaven, perhaps the Israelis should make the appropriate arrangements. That, in fact, is the only way to deal with Hizbullah, Hamas and Islamic Jihad. These are not people with whom you can reason, much less negotiate.

No matter what is done to them, unless Hizbullah is thoroughly exterminated, or made to suffer such pain as to compel them think twice about another war with Israel – an almost impossible task – they will reappear, rearm and renew the terrorism.

For Israel to withdraw from Lebanon without a clear and

decisive victory over Hizbullah would be an historic tragedy, a mortal blow to the heart of Israel and give aid and comfort to every terrorist. I don't know if Israel could survive such a psychological calamity. Remember Hamas bragging how they forced 8,000 Jewish settlers to flee Gaza? It scored them control of the Palestinian Authority. Now, imagine Hizbullah declaring that it had fought the mighty Israeli war machine, "and we are still here!" Hizbullah must be utterly and completely destroyed like the metastatic cancer it is.

For the Record

July 28, 2006

To the Editor (JP):

The news from Europe was not so good. At a press conference at the conclusion of the Rome Conference, Secretary of State Condoleezza Rice stood by herself at the side of the stage holding her head as if she were suffering from a pounding migraine headache. The EU ministers and the UN's Kofi Annan – who was more concerned about Israel's so-called excesses than his UNIFIL troops practically cohabiting with Hizbullah – cried crocodile tears for Lebanese civilians and urged an immediate cease-fire in Lebanon without acknowledging what that would portend. It was then clear that America, with England, Canada and Australia, stood alone with Israel in the knowledge that the Hizbullah monster had to die. That's what gave Secretary Rice "Excedrin Headache #1": stupid allies.

The EU, and particularly the UN, still do not get it. Lebanon is not about the two kidnapped and eight murdered Israeli soldiers. It is not about Hizbullah or even Lebanon. Whatever else the Middle East wars have been about in the past, we are at the beginning of a new chapter: This war is about Iran and hegemony. Hizbullah are merely the actors and Lebanon is merely the current venue.

The cross-border assault against Israel was, for all intents and purposes, carried out by Iran. Of course, Syria was involved, but Syria is merely the remora at the side of the Iranian shark. One dirty look from Ahmadinejad and young Assad would fold like the cheap suit he is.

When Hizbullah crossed Israel's border, it was a test of Israeli Prime Minister Olmert's backbone. But when Hizbullah started firing thousands of rockets and missiles into not just northern Israel but also Haifa, Israel's third largest city, it became a test of American, EU and UN backbone. Israel's fundamentally aerial response was entirely reasonable under the circumstances. (Frankly, I don't know why the IDF hasn't moved into Lebanon with its ground forces, which are necessary to put Hizbullah out of commission. But that's a different issue for now.) Israel responded fairly to Hizbullah's act of war.

The problem is that this is a war unlike those fought in 1956, 1967 and 1973. Hizbullah terrorists are spread out over a vast area with equipment and weaponry that can be hidden under a car... or in a hospital, apartment house, school or under a tree. This is not a war that can be won in a few days or even weeks. And that is another problem. People expect the IDF to end wars within a few weeks or a month, because of past successes, albeit under completely different circumstances. And because Hizbullah is hiding among the civilian population – a clear violation of the Geneva Convention – as well as beside the UNIFIL forces, Israel's job will take longer to complete and more civilians are going to die. So now the Europeans have seen enough. They want a ceasefire in spite of the fact that doing so before Hizbullah is cut down to size means, among other things, that Israel will have to fight this war again.

But that isn't what brought on the secretary's migraine headache. It is the realization that has come to Bush, Rice and UN Ambassador Bolton that this war is a test of the West's ability and willingness to fight Iran. As the Egyptians, Jordanians and even the Saudis understand, a strong, heavily militarized terrorist organization operating with a sovereign's support is, for now, the primary threat to stability in the Middle East.

In fact, Ahmadinejad is testing Europe more than he is testing Israel. Iran already has missiles that could reach Israel. It just doesn't have the "proper" payload to do maximum damage at this time. In a few years – and no one is particularly sure when – Iran will have both a nuclear capability and the means to deliver its payload into Western Europe. Ahmadinejad is patting himself on the back as Europe backs down again. Imagine his boldness when Iran's military is nuclear capable. He will be positively giddy, and the Europeans will be shaking in their basements.

Churchill understood why it was necessary to stop Hitler at Munich. No one else did and the consequence of the ostriches sticking their heads in the sand was World War II. The Iranians have already declared their intentions to "wipe Israel off the face of the Earth," to destroy America, and to establish an Islamic caliphate from Iran to Spain. Lebanon is the first real test of Iranian hegemony. Europe must come to understand that if they don't now fight back in the Middle East, they may well find themselves and all of Europe under Iranian nuclear threat. And then they can appease radical Islam from the comfort of their own homes.

Madmen are in charge of the asylum. In time they will also be in control of missile silos. The Europeans close their eyes to this threat at their own peril.

We shouldn't stop the Israelis. We should be right there covering their backs.

August 7, 2006

To the Editor (JP):

Re: "Lebanese PM Reverses Claim of 40 Dead" and "The Media War." Against a background of rhetoric, hyperbole and outright lies, Lebanon's Prime Minister Fouad Siniora declared that Israel's belligerence has set Lebanon back 50 years. It is apparently of no moment that the destruction in Lebanon is the direct consequence of the Lebanese having turned their government over to terrorists who have a stake in seeing more, rather than fewer, civilians die.

In the face of uncontroverted evidence that Hizbullah has manipulated the international media's coverage in Lebanon, what's left of the Lebanese government continues to be well practiced in the art of deception. Last week, in a televised speech to an emergency meeting of the Organization of the Islamic Conference, Mr. Siniora declared that 900 Lebanese had been killed. In fact, the real number is closer to half that because the figures from the Lebanese Health Ministry include not only confirmed deaths but also those who are missing.

Mr. Siniora also declared that more than a million Lebanese had been displaced. According to even the UN – whose anti-Israel animus is well-documented – the real number is half of that.

Following the Israeli raid on Houla, Siniora and Nasrallah referred to the "massacre" of 40 civilians. The Israelis, it was published, had committed "war crimes." Today, however, Siniora admitted that only one person died.

Now it comes out that Reuters published a photo of Beirut doctored in such a way as to make it appear that damage caused by Israel was far more severe than it actually was. This comes within two weeks of CNN admitting that it allowed Hizbullah to take a reporter and camera crew into Beirut, but that CNN could film only what Hizbullah wanted the world to see. CNN's reporter acknowledged that no effort was made to ascertain the truth of what Hizbullah had CNN represent to the world.

That mendacity should parade around the world as fact is

bad enough. Managed news is neither new nor news. But what is more disturbing is that the world is so ready to accept as fact any blood libel of which Israel is accused. Again, the Israelis are portrayed as heartless monsters and the Arabs as innocents.

Why is the world so eager to accept as truth every accusation hurled against the Israelis? Why is it that knowing full well both that the Israelis have taken casualties in order to protect Arab civilians and that Arab anti-Semitism heaps one breathtaking lie upon another, every anti-Israel utterance still passes international muster?

The failure to greet rhetoric, hyperbole and mendacity with skepticism is not the result of trust or naivete. Rather, it is the result of a predisposition to believe the worst of a people that has only asked to be left alone to make its paradise in the desert. There is a word for it and you will find it in the commandment that God should have written but did not: Thou shall not hate.

Israel and the Palestinians – What the Media Aren't Telling You

August 15, 2006

To the Editor (WSJ):

The answer to who will disarm Hizbullah is on everyone's lips: No one. The UN's international peacekeeping force led by the courageous French? With the same detachment with which Claude Reins intoned in *Casablanca* that "Major Strasser has been shot. Round up the usual suspects," UNIFIL's French commander, Maj. Gen. Alain Pellegrini, demurs that Hizbullah is an internal Lebanese matter; the 15,000 UN troops under his command will not get involved. Lebanese Defense Minister Elias Murr has wasted no time in declaring that the Lebanese Army will not ask Hizbullah to hand over its weapons.

Disarm Hizbullah? The Lebanese won't do it. The UN won't do it. The Israelis have been waved away. So much for the keystone to peace in Lebanon. The suggestion that Hizbullah had become a "state within a state" no longer holds true, and it is now Lebanon that bears that distinction.

What remains is not just Hizbullah or even Syria. They are merely drones. The Iranians have learned that the current Israeli government does not have the stomach for combat and, failing that, the US can't make Olmert grow a spine.

Except in the unlikely event Israel presses the point, one shouldn't expect Hizbullah to reengage the Israelis any time soon. There will, of course, be a follow-up to this war; with the same dramatis personae, albeit with a slight variation. Iran has learned all it needs to know from the machinations of the past weekend and will be content to have Hizbullah rearm for now. Then, when it suits Iran's purpose, Hizbullah and perhaps Syria will fabricate a grievance and initiate the next Arab-Israeli confrontation.

And when will it suit Iran's purpose? There are so many potential tripwires in the Middle East that it is hard to pinpoint any specific event. Perhaps when Israel is again engaged in Gaza. Perhaps when Hamas establishes a more substantial foothold in the West Bank. Or perhaps when Iran has a nuclear weapon.

Then, when Iran tells the West what to do with Israel, there will be more than arrogance behind its threat to "wipe Israel off the face of the Earth."

August 16, 2006

To the Editor (JP):

From the very beginning it was understood, not just by the Lebanese, Israelis, Americans and Europeans, but the Arab League as well, that Hizbullah had to be disarmed for peace to return to Lebanon. Not once, but twice in two years, the Security Council has demanded, by Resolution 1559 in 2004 and again only four days ago by Resolution 1701, the military neutralization of Hizbullah.

The disarming of Hizbullah is now to be accomplished by 15,000 Lebanese troops, most of whom side with Hizbullah, and another 15,000 troops made up of a multinational UN force under French command. Four events in the last day make it clear that this new resolution is another United Nations charade, that Israel has again been sandbagged, that Hizbullah will retain its weapons, that this cease-fire is a canard, and that the power, both real and perceived, of Iran has risen sharply.

First, the French leader of the UN's 15,000 troops, Maj. Gen. Pellegrini, has demurred that Hizbullah is an internal Lebanese matter; the 15,000 UN troops under his command will not get involved.

Second, Lebanese Defense Minister Elias Murr has declared that the Lebanese Army will not ask Hizbullah to hand over its weapons. The Lebanese, he sneers, will not do Israel's job.

Third, Hizbullah declared that it would not disarm, thus relieving the Lebanese Army and UN troops of the embarrassment of trying to do something they could not accomplish.

Fourth are reports of an agreement between Hizbullah and the Lebanese government that Hizbullah will not have to surrender its arms, a flagrant violation of Resolution 1701.

After all the death and pain, nothing has dramatically changed. All the "what ifs" – What if Israel had moved its ground forces in after the first week of fighting? What if the international community hadn't abandoned Israel? What if Syria and Iran had been engaged? – are now irrelevant. Perhaps Israel should have known that nothing out of the UN would redound to her benefit, but I'm not sure Israel really had any choice after Secretary Rice backpedaled and pressed for a cease-fire.

Significantly, neither Iran nor Syria, the playwrights in this Theater of Insanity, paid any price for their perfidy. Reports are already coming in that the Syrians have already started to send new weapons into south Lebanon. Resolution 1701, which doesn't mention Iran or Syria, virtually transfers Israel's right of self-defense to Secretary General Annan, another player who loves her not. And so another resolution lies to rot in the UN sewer of impotence and contempt for Israel.

Israel and the Palestinians – What the Media Aren't Telling You

September 10, 2006

To the Editor (Newsday):

News this past week that America is pressuring Israel to release a senior terrorist "with blood on his hands" flies in the face of the Bush Doctrine, which says: "You're either with us or you're with the terrorists." (It is, moreover, perplexing that this news was not carried by any of the major newspapers or wire services. What journalistic objective was served by America's mainstream media burying this story?)

Mahmoud Damra, who was appointed only this past June to lead Force 17, President Abbas's personal security unit, was arrested last week by Israeli forces in the West Bank. Since 2000, Damra had led the Al Aksa Martyrs Brigade in Ramallah, which has carried out many fatal attacks upon Israelis, including shootings, attacks on settlers and planting roadside bombs.

Perhaps it is of no small import to the US that Abbas has personally demanded Damra's release as integral to his own personal safety. America tries to bolster Abbas, who plays the moderate in the Hamas-Fatah charade of "good cop, bad cop." But the question seemingly overlooked is what Damra's release would mean, not to the peace process, which is dead, but to the state of peace in Judea, Samaria and the rest of Israel.

As has long been the case with terrorists released from Israeli prisons, Damra will resume his murderous partnership with death, this time from the sanctity of the Palestinian president's inner circle.

The question for the secretary of state is why would America want Damra, and therefore murder, unleashed? What purpose is served by obtaining the freedom of a man whose life is dedicated to the destruction of not just Israel, but of America as well? And what message are we sending the Israelis who risk their lives to capture such a man?

For the Record

September 30, 2006

To the Editor (NYT):

Your editorial "Out of the Mouth of Aides" (Sept. 30, 2006) fails to understand the discontent in the Middle East by wrongfully attempting to define all enmity in terms of Israel and the Palestinians. Internecine Arab conflict has a long history preceding by millennia the establishment of the State of Israel.

Worse yet is your willingness to sacrifice Israel in the naive expectation that America will be accepted by radical Muslims. Cutting Israel loose would place Israel in existential jeopardy, and to do so to appease people who demand America's death is both self-delusional and historically deficient.

What "further compromises" would you demand of Israel? Recognizing a Palestinian "right of return" would be suicide and both Gaza and Lebanon have plunged a sword through the heart of "land for peace."

It is also fallacious to argue that progress on the Israeli-Palestinian conflict is the *sine qua non* for obtaining Arab "cooperation" on the Iranian front. The Saudi royals know, as do Jordan's king and Egypt's president, that the most serious geopolitical threat in the Middle East emanates from Iran and her support of numerous radical-Islamist terrorist militias. The concept of linkage is irrelevant and will dangerously delay serious efforts to preempt and contain a pre-nuclear Iran. The rest of it – reviving peace talks, propping up of Abbas, targeted killings and "a halt of all settlement construction" – is just background noise.

Israel and the Palestinians – What the Media Aren't Telling You

October 18, 2006

To the Editor (JP):

Concerning the massive buildup of arms in Gaza (October 17, 2006), one must be deeply troubled by Defense Minister Peretz's decision not to introduce ground troops and to let diplomacy solve the problem. It was precisely such a failure to engage on the ground, only eight weeks ago, that cost Israel so dearly in the recent Lebanese conflict.

His "decision" reminded me of something that happened last week. I awoke in the middle of the night and went downstairs for a glass of cold milk. When I opened the container I could smell that it had gone sour. I threw it out. I didn't put it back in the refrigerator, close the door and say "Maybe it will be better in the morning." When something doesn't work, you throw it out.

What has diplomacy brought to Israel in the last year? "Land for peace" in Gaza? More arms have been brought into Gaza in the last year than in the preceding 58 years. The Hamas-run government, even in the face of severe sanctions, holds true to its goal of destroying Israel and proudly declares its fitness to deal the IDF a crushing blow. President Abbas has been so frustrated at every turn in his efforts to end the anarchy in Gaza that he tries – unsuccessfully – to form a unity government with Hamas. Missiles and rockets continue to be fired daily from Gaza into pre-1967 Israel. Syria continues to arm Hizbullah. And against this history of failure, Secretary Rice wastes one effort after another to get the Arabs to stop the mayhem; all to no effect. Resolution 1701 has failed to disarm Hizbullah. Resolution 1701 has failed to seal the Lebanese-Syrian border. Resolution 1701 has failed to bring either Ehud Goldwasser or Eldad Regev back from captivity. And the Lebanese reply to Prime Minister Olmert's offer to discuss peace face-to-face and unconditionally has received the rebuke that "Lebanon will be the *last* Arab country that could sign a peace agreement with Israel."

Against this massive stone wall of failure, for Mr. Peretz to rely on diplomacy to resolve the conflict in Gaza demonstrates a suicidal ability to ignore reality and abandon Israel's well-being to wishful thinking. His policy may play in a university debate, but it falls with a sickening thud when coming from the minister of defense. Mr. Peretz may well exemplify Pope's observation that "hope springs eternal from the human breast," but from where I sit, he keeps putting sour milk back in the refrigerator.

Israel and the Palestinians – What the Media Aren't Telling You

November 1, 2006

To the Editor (NYT):

Today's Op-Ed ("Pause for Peace") by a senior adviser to Hamas Prime Minister Haniya is troubling on a number of levels, not the least of which is that the *Times*, the so-called "paper of record," gave this mendacious, murderous gang prominent space to camouflage its pathology.

First, Mr. Yousef disguises genocidal intent behind words of peace and trust. He is correct that we know where Hamas stands. Since its violent nascence in 1987, it has unapologetically advanced its *raison d'être*: the destruction of Israel.

Second, it is most telling that Mr. Yousef proposes a *hudna* – which he describes as a 10-year period of peace, negotiation and reconciliation. (It is worth noting that in 622 CE, Mohammed was forced to flee the city of Quraysh for Medina. By 628 CE, Mohammed's forces in Medina were sufficiently strong as to enable him to enter into the Treaty of Hudaybiya, which provided for a ten-year truce with Quraysh. As soon as the truce was signed, Mohammed armed his followers and formed new alliances such that he was able to toss aside Quraysh entreaties to not break the truce. In January 630, Mohammed defeated the Quraysh and took over their city, Mecca, without a fight. On May 10, 1994, Arafat deflected Arab criticism by explaining that the accords were "no more than the agreement signed by our Prophet Mohammed and the Quraysh in Mecca.")

What exposes his plan as a Trojan horse is that Mr. Yousef does not sue for peace. Thus, Hamas seeks a cease-fire with Israel only to train and arm itself with high quality weapons from Hizbullah, Iran and Syria, all traveling through Egypt and Lebanon. And perhaps it is also because at the core of Hamas's charter is a Middle East caliphate without Israel and Jews.

Finally, Mr. Yousef's analogy to the cease-fire between the IRA and Britain is contemptibly disingenuous. While the IRA engaged in violence to end what it termed Britain's "occupation" of Northern Ireland, it never demanded the destruction of Britain.

To paraphrase Shakespeare in *Richard III*, heed not their honeyed words. They are merely old wine in new bottles.

Israel and the Palestinians – What the Media Aren't Telling You

December 15, 2006

To the Editor (NYT):

Rev. Ralph Roy's letter (Dec. 15, 2006) asks "Why can't we be pro-Israel and pro-Palestinian at the same time?" This is a seemingly reasonable question which, however, cannot withstand moral or reasoned scrutiny.

The answer to his question lies in the actions and intentions of each side. The Israelis want to be left alone and live in peace with all. The Palestinian terrorists want to kill Jews. Specifically, Palestinian children are indoctrinated to hate Jews as they are taught to read, while Israeli children are just taught to read. Palestinian children are exposed in school, home and mosque to murderous incitement, while Israeli children are exposed to Torah, literature and science. Fanatic Palestinian mothers proudly send their children off to die in order to kill Jews. Israeli mothers cherish and nurture theirs. Israelis hold peace marches. Palestinians organize to provoke terror. Israelis export medical technology while the Palestinians export death.

There is no moral equivalence and that is why I am pro-Israel and cannot be pro-Palestinian, and I find it odd that a man of God fails to grasp the distinction.

For the Record

January 18, 2007

To the Editor (Newsday):

Steven Cook's 1/17/07 Op-Ed ("US Repeating Mideast Mistakes?"), while correctly addressing the threat of Iranian hegemony in Judea, Samaria and Gaza, mistakenly urges Secretary Rice to focus on matters that would in fact perpetuate the Israeli-Palestinian impasse.

Mr. Cook suggests "working with" (read coercing) Israel toward the release of prisoners, especially women and children. In so doing, Mr. Cook wrongfully creates an equivalency between those in Israeli jails for having committed crimes of terrorism and the kidnapping of Israeli soldiers by terrorists. It is noteworthy that virtually all released terrorists return to terrorism, usually immediately.

Next, he urges "supporting a political horizon for Palestinian statehood." The problems with that are too numerous to list here, but we can start with the issue of terrorism. The Palestinian Authority is considerably further away from eliminating the terrorists – its first obligation under the Road Map – than it was last year. Indeed, Hamas controls the government and the streets.

Moreover, only last week, President Abbas, with nary a protest from the US, made a strong speech in which he demanded that the Palestinians turn their guns away from each other and toward the Israelis. His encouragement of terrorism is a course least likely to instill confidence in Jerusalem.

Iran is the foremost threat to regional stability and international peace. But the solution lies not in Jerusalem, but the Arab capitals.

Israel and the Palestinians – What the Media Aren't Telling You

February 9, 2007

To the Editor (Newsday):

The "unity government" in Gaza, announced yesterday from Saudi Arabia, brings a combination of relief and apprehension. The cease-fire in Gaza is a significant accomplishment. It stops, for the time being, the bloody civil war being waged between the partisans of President Abbas, leader of the Fatah terrorists, and those of Prime Minister Ismail Haniyeh, the leader of the Hamas terrorists. It is, however, likely to have the same resonance as one hand clapping.

To bring a halt to the internecine mayhem is itself a worthy deed. But a "unity government" suggests that Fatah and Hamas will share power in the PA to a degree and manner which both are willing to accept. That is, they will rule hand in hand with common objectives. I emphasize "common."

This unity government is merely old wine in new bottles. Before Mecca, the Palestinians had a government comprised of a Hamas-dominated legislature and a Fatah-dominated executive, with ministries under the control of one party or the other. What has Mecca brought us? The Hamas-Fatah-Palestinian Authority is structured much as it was before; the same legislature and the same executives. Perhaps the apportionment of ministries will vary a little, yet the crucial Interior Ministry, which controls the police and "army," is still up for grabs. Whether the Interior is occupied at the top by Hamas's bloody Sayed Said or Fatah strongman Muhammad Dahlan, the fact is likely to remain that the guns will owe their allegiance not to the PA, but to Hamas, Fatah and the Popular Resistance Committees. Leopards don't change their spots so casually, and this "new" government is still a wolf in wolves' clothing.

Sadly, most of the Western bloc is taking a wait-and-see attitude with the "new" PA. In terms of both the Israeli-Palestinian conflict and regional stability, the most important consequence of Mecca was the adamant refusal of Hamas to give so much as a hint of reformation of its constitutional *raison d'être*, the destruction of

Israel. No renunciation of terrorism, no recognition of Israel, and no agreement to abide by past Palestinian-Israeli treaties.

The consequence of all this is that what little was left of Mahmoud Abbas has been eviscerated. Fatah was the first to blink. Hamas has returned triumphant and its star continues to rise. Now Hamas controls the guns. And the guns control the streets.

It is perhaps only a perverse benefit that has risen from the ashes of Gaza – unlike Fatah, Hamas does not mince its words or lie to the West to tell us what we want to hear. Contrary to the words of Secretary of State Rice, Abbas is, and always has been, an enemy of Israel and the United States. As the architect of the Achille Lauro affair and the financier of the 1972 massacre at the Munich Olympics, its peace dialogues have thinly disguised a murderous intent.

Recall that the first obligation of the Palestinians under the now-deceased Road Map was to end terrorism. I do not for one nanosecond believe that Abbas, with armed forces of many tens of thousands, was unable to stop the firing of rockets and missiles from Gaza. Virtually every single day since Israel "disengaged" from Gaza some 18 months ago, the Gazans have fired missile after missile into pre-1967 Israel. Children have died while Prime Minister Olmert tap danced on egg shells and tightened the reins on the IDF. When Israel finally did enter Gaza, it was only after IDF soldier Gilad Shalit had been kidnapped. Hundreds of bodies later, Shalit is still in Gaza and the missiles keep coming. In his call for an end to the civil war, Abbas ecumenically asked the Palestinians to stop shooting each other and to fire instead on the Israelis.

Let's sum it up. The guns have stopped – for now – but insofar as the constituent parts of the PA are concerned, this new unity government doesn't even qualify as old wine in new bottles. It is run by Hamas. And Hamas, though lacking Abbas's subtle, false treachery, freely admits, as if it were a virtue, that one way or the other Israel must be destroyed. The gift of the Saudis is that Mecca is likely to be the prelude to an internecine battle for the hearts and minds – not to mention the bodies – of the Palestinians.

More than 30 years ago, Hafez al-Assad ordered the murder of 20,000 Palestinians in the Syrian city of Hama. The catchphrase in the Middle East then was "Hama Rules." Not so different now in Gaza; Hamas rules.

For the Record

March 13, 2007

To the Editor (NYT):

The news that the United Nations Human Rights Council plans to open a permanent file on Israel for violations of international law until she withdraws from "occupied" Palestinian lands to the pre-1967 borders smacks of moral decomposition and hypocrisy.

It is worth noting that since its inception, the UNHRC has issued only eight resolutions, every one of which was directed against Israel. It has also held three special sessions…all on Israel.

In a world where genocide has become commonplace on the African continent, "honor killings", sectarian warfare and suicide-murder pervade the Middle East, Kim Jong Il maintains a murderous nuclear dictatorship in North Korea and non-Muslims are prohibited from entering the city of Mecca, the council's poisonous obsession with Israel deprives it of credibility and moral authority.

March 26, 2007

To the Editor (NYT):

Your editorial "The Hamas Conundrum" correctly points out that the singular obstruction to peace talks is Palestinian violence. However, by continuing to urge resumption of negotiations on the basis of "land for peace," you erroneously place the burden back on Israel. Moreover, the experience with Gaza should have put a knife through the heart of the "land for peace" theory.

If a peace process is to take place, it can only get out of the starting gate by the total and permanent cessation of terrorism. Yet, even if the Palestinians continue their modified *hudna*, there are many of us who believe it would be a mere charade in furtherance of the Palestinian plan for the staged destruction of Israel.

Meanwhile, Hamas leaders proudly insist they will destroy Israel. What is the conundrum?

For the Record

29 March 2007

To the Editor (Ha'aretz),

Reading "Two Gaza Militants Seriously Hurt in IAF Strike on Qassam Launchers", I was immediately struck by your ubiquitous reference to terrorists as "militants" and other nonviolent terms.

For example, the very first sentence refers to "a group of militants preparing to fire Qassam rockets into Israel..." In fact, throughout the piece, Palestinian terrorists are also identified variously as a "Qassam-launching squad, "armed men," and a "suicide-bomber who carried out an attack on French Hill in Jerusalem in September 2004, killing two border policemen."

By referring to terrorists as merely militants or armed men, you sanitize their murderous conduct by making it sound like a campus demonstration. To characterize their actions like a political rally does a gross disservice to your readers and insults the memory of those who have died at the terrorists' bloodied hands. I am stunned that a prominent Israeli newspaper should use its power and influence in such a "politically correct" manner.

And those two dead policemen in Jerusalem were not merely "attacked." They were murdered. Do you have any objection to the words "murderer" and "killer," which in fact more accurately convey the true nature of the "militants"?

This is the sort of journalism I have come to expect from Reuters and the BBC, but never from an Israeli publication whose responsibility to its country and countrymen – not to mention the world – demands that you tell the truth.

May 2, 2007

To the Editor (NYT):

Today's editorial ("A Harsh, Healthy Verdict in Israel"), while correctly pointing out the errors of Israel's Second Lebanon War, wrongly posits that peace cannot be won militarily without "a more active diplomacy…and a willingness to take risks." Yet, recent history is replete with instances of Israel being battered for taking such risks.

Israel's unilateral withdrawal from Lebanon made possible the militarization of southern Lebanon and the rise of Hizbullah. Recognition of the PLO at Oslo brought about the so-called Aksa intifada with its sustained suicide bombings. Withdrawal from Gaza, again unilateral, brought massive and uncontrolled weapons smuggling and a Hamas government – whose acting speaker of the Palestinian Legislative Council this past Friday called for the annihilation of all Americans and Israelis "down to the very last one." The "uncertain possibilities for peace" have become the size of a quark.

With its government on the brink of implosion and the Palestinians calling daily for her destruction, Israel cannot afford further Arab indulgences. Appeasement always comes at a price disproportionate to its insignificant benefit.

For the Record

May 9, 2007

To the Editor (JP):

It is odd of US Congressman Ackerman to criticize an effort to clear away some of the smoke, which is all the refugee problem is inasmuch as Israel, as an existential matter, can never accept them. There are some demands which are so preposterous as to require their being utterly ignored. The so-called "right of return" is one such issue. Does Mr. Ackerman believe, for example, that Israel should sit down with Hamas, which demands the death of all of Israel's Jews and destruction of the state? Should those matters be "on the table" in the interest of letting the players handle their own cards?

Some issues, such as life or death ones, are nonnegotiable. For a Jewish congressman, of all people, to suggest otherwise is a pathetic exercise in obsequiousness and political correctness. I am disappointed that Mr. Ackerman lacks the backbone to tell the Palestinians that our right to exist is not – and never will be – on the table.

Israel and the Palestinians – What the Media Aren't Telling You

May 25, 2007

To the Editor (NYT),

Your report today on Israel's arrests of 33 Palestinians correctly describes it as an escalation of Israel's response to the daily onslaught of rocket fire from Gaza. Until this past week, the Israelis, not wishing to escalate the conflict, essentially sat on their hands while rocket after rocket flew into Sderot,

However, it is misleading to report only that Hamas resumed rocket fire 10 days ago. Almost every day since a cease-fire was declared six months ago, other Palestinian terrorists –most notably Islamic Jihad – have fired rockets against an entirely civilian population. Indeed, Palestinians have been striking at Sderot from Gaza with virtual impunity for more than five years.

Unfortunately, Israel's forbearance in response to international pressure was read by the Palestinians as weakness. No other country would tolerate rocket fire across an international border, much less directed at civilians. And no other country would be expected to sit back and just take it. Thus, Hamas's entry into the fray comes as no surprise.

May 31, 2007

To the Editor (NYT):

Your report today ("Jihadist Groups Fill a Palestinian Power Vacuum,") is perhaps most noteworthy for the revelation that the terrorism and anarchy consuming Gaza have left an important Palestinian distraught – a senior member of Hamas. Mr. Taha decries what has become of his people at the hands of fundamentalists preaching violence.

For generations, the Palestinians have raised their children to hate and kill Jews as they embrace death. Tolerance and respect for others has been discarded in favor of schools and camps which inculcate rabid prejudice and teach children to hate Jews and how to kill them. What did Mr. Taha think would come of such an education in such a culture? The Palestinians are reaping what they have sowed, but the danger is not what they may do to themselves, but what they intend to do to the rest of us.

It is remarkable that Mr. Taha is surprised at what his people have created. On the other hand, so was Dr. Frankenstein.

June 8, 2007

To the Editor (US News & World Report):

Larry Derfner's report ("Jerusalem Undivided" 6/3/07) barely contains his displeasure with the Israelis and only begrudgingly concedes the transcendence of Israel's culture over that of the Palestinians.

Mr. Derfner wastes no time in expressing his bias when he declares that Israel "seized" Arab Jerusalem in 1967. Is it possible that he is unfamiliar with the Six Day War? Or is it irrelevant that the Jordanians would to this day control east Jerusalem had they not ignored Israel's warning to stay out of the war? Perhaps it is not relevant either that it was Jordan that seized Arab Jerusalem in violation of international law after the War of Independence in 1948. Be that as it may, Israel's control of a united Jerusalem is a right earned under the laws of war and peace, and under which all residents are free to practice their religion and visit their holy sites; something denied to Jerusalem's Jews under the Jordanian occupation.

When Mr. Derfner says that "Israel has cracked down on Jerusalem Arab political activity since the intifada uprising in 2000," he makes the intifada sound like a march or a pep rally. The intifada brought rioting and murder. The murder of civilians at that. Suicide bombers and weapons are smuggled in ambulances marked with the Red Cross. Arab women and children are packed with explosives to kill Israeli women and children. Israeli schools are targets. Cafes, even in heavily Arab Haifa, are blown up. These were the choices the Palestinians made for themselves. The Israeli response was entirely defensive.

Similarly, Mr. Derfner's characterization of the PA's performance as "dismal" is understatement at its best. Gaza has become a killing ground for the competing Palestinian gangs, clans, "security" forces and prevailing "committees." People are afraid to walk the streets in Gaza. Children are killed in demonstrations and are caught in the cross-fire. Anarchy, chaos, murder, terror and squalor. All brought to Gaza by the Palestinians themselves.

That Jerusalem's Arabs are voting for Israel with their feet is irrefutable evidence that they finally see their countrymen for what they are. Jerusalem's Arabs see what is happening in Gaza and grasp the fact that Palestinian despondency and poverty is the result, not of Israeli "occupation," but, rather, of Palestinian treachery and its culture of death. The security wall and the checkpoints are all the consequence of Palestinian efforts to kill Israelis. Mr. Derfner's *ipse dixit* is neither correct nor compelling. "Hell in Jerusalem"? Not by a long shot.

Golda Meir was right when she said that there would be no peace until the Arabs loved their children more than they hated the Israelis. At last it seems some of them finally get it.

Israel and the Palestinians – What the Media Aren't Telling You

June 14, 2007

To the Editor (IJP):

With the descent of Gaza into a full-blown civil war as Hamas moves to complete its *coup d'ètat*, the Palestinians are giving the rest of the world a good taste of what they're made of – and what the Israelis have been facing all these years. In recent days we have witnessed men executed in front of their wives and children. Men handcuffed and pushed over the roof of an 18-story building. A man decapitated by being shot in the head 40 times by high-powered rifles. Gangland-style executions. It gets worse.

Many examples abound but are too numerous to recount here; so let us begin with the sick. Hamas gunmen have murdered people in hospitals. When two pro-Fatah clan women tried to take a sick girl to a hospital, Hamas gunmen killed both of them. Hamas would not even hold their fire long enough for a hospital with no water to restore electricity. To the mind of these Palestinians, there are no innocents.

Such blood-lust, sadly, is not limited to the male of the species. It was recently reported that the Israelis intercepted and arrested two Palestinian women on their way to carry out a suicide mission. That the would-be suicide bombers were women is not particularly noteworthy, nor is the fact that their intended victims were civilians. No, what distinguishes these two women goes to the Palestinians' ability to destroy what nature provides, i.e., the instinct of a mother. One of the women has three children. She believed that loving, protecting, raising and nurturing her children was less important than killing some Jews.

The second woman brings a distinction previously unknown to the Palestinian culture of hatred. This woman was nine months' pregnant! Think about that for a minute. Let it sink in, and try not to shudder at its unspeakable inhumanity. It is bad enough that a mother would abandon her children for the sake of spilling Jewish blood. But it is quite another kettle of fish for a woman to destroy – and in so wanton and heartless a manner – the baby she carries in her body. Its sheer, unrelenting fanaticism, devoid of compassion, leaves the mind numb.

That world opinion should prefer the Palestinians to the Israelis is, from an objective view, unfathomable. When English unions, educators and journalists take up the Palestinians and elect to boycott the Israelis, one searches for a rational explanation. In vain.

Israel and the Palestinians – What the Media Aren't Telling You

June 15, 2007

To the Editor (NYT):

Your editorial ("Palestinians at War" June 15), while correctly assessing the damage to the Gazans and the reconstituted Palestinian Authority, mistakenly places the burden on the Israelis to save Abbas and the PA.

If Gaza taught us anything, it was that the Palestinians, left to their own devices, are as yet incapable of creating their own free society, whether as a republic, democracy or even with a benign despot.

The barrier to Palestinian normalicy lies not with Israel's removal of blockades and checkpoints and the release of millions of dollars to the PA. There are no checkpoints in Gaza. There are no Israelis in Gaza. In the past year the PA received more foreign aid than it did in the year prior to the election of Hamas. Israel transferred $100 million to the PA in December in an effort to prop up Fatah. Curiously, that vast fund has somehow disappeared.

To aid Abbas in fighting Hamas, millions of bullets, RPGs, AK-47s, M-16s, armored vehicles, mortars and hand grenades were all sent to the PA, yet found their way to Hamas. Peace in Judea and Samaria, as was the case with Gaza, is the responsibility of the Palestinians alone. Israel cannot stop them from killing each other or make them accept the sanctity of life.

For the Record

June 18, 2007

To the Editor (NYT):

Adam LaBor's Op-Ed ("New Lyrics for Israel" June 18, 2007) urges a core change to Israel's national anthem by changing the reference from a "Jewish" soul to an "Israeli" soul. Noting that 20% of Israel's population is not Jewish, Mr. LaBor advocates this change as "a gesture of inclusion" and in the name of "religious diversity." His is a thinly veiled effort to exorcize the Jewish identity from the Jewish state.

Mr. LaBor's search for inclusion and diversity is disingenuous. An attempt to deprive Israel of its Jewish soul means the dejudaization of Israel. It is a transparent effort to deny by *ipse dixit* the Jewish soul that has existed in Judea and Samaria for over 3,000 years, and a preliminary step toward delegitimizing the Jewish state, from which point it will be argued that there is neither reason nor right for a Jewish state to even exist.

Finally, his closing statement that the non-Jewish population is "here to stay" is no more than a condescending poke in the eye. As if by sleight of hand, Mr. LaBor dismisses a fact he himself acknowledges, i.e., 80% of Israel's population *is* Jewish. And they, too, are "here to stay."

Israel and the Palestinians – What the Media Aren't Telling You

June 20, 2007

To the Editor (Newsday):

This week's events have seen Sec'y Rice recognize the reconstituted Palestinian Authority, announce a plan to release over $125 million in direct and non-direct aid to the new PA in the West Bank, and President Bush and Prime Minister Olmert congratulate each other for being masters of their domains. I fear the congratulations are premature.

What has happened in Gaza in the last two weeks is nothing to celebrate. Gaza is now under the control of Islamic terrorists. The PA president led the retreat from Gaza to the West Bank. The Gaza-Egypt border remains a sieve through which a veritable army of terrorists and weapons casually passes. Only parts of the West Bank are under the control of the PA, whose main instrument of domestic diplomacy remains the murderous Al Aksa Martyrs Brigades. Major cities such as Nablus, Hebron and Jenin remain Hamas strongholds. And Kassam rockets continue to be fired from Gaza.

And last, but not least, the PA is still run by Mahmoud Abbas, Arafat's right hand for about 40 years, who – even before Hamas was elected 18 months ago – didn't lift a finger to end the terrorism coming from either Gaza or the West Bank. It is revealing that Abbas has condemned terrorism only because it doesn't play well in the international media to see Israeli children blown up; not that killing Israelis is wrong, mind you, but that it doesn't advance the Palestinian cause.

It is worth noting that instead of summoning the PA security forces – which he urged America and Israel to arm and train – he has sent the bloodthirsty Al Aksa Martyrs Brigades to patrol the West Bank.

In the face of a laundry list of failures, why are Bush and Olmert talking about negotiating final status issues? Why has Abbas suddenly become America's and the Israeli Left's golden boy? Too much is happening too fast, and with little or no reflection on what has happened and no thought of what consequences await us.

Hamas now controls Gaza and parts of the West Bank. Anyone who thinks that the blood lust of Hamas, Hizbullah, Iran and Syria is now sated is fooling himself. It's way too early to be slapping each other on the back. The Israeli-Palestinian conflict isn't over. Not by a long shot.

Israel and the Palestinians – What the Media Aren't Telling You

June 26, 2007

To the Editor (Newsday):

Re: Israel Agrees to Release Funds to Abbas (6/26/07): If the road to hell is paved with good intentions, Prime Minister Olmert's arrival in the nether world can be expected to be smooth and soon. News that he intends to release hundreds of millions of dollars to the PA as well as hundreds of Palestinians in Israeli jails – after signing an agreement to foreswear terrorism – makes Neville Chamberlain's behavior at Munich look like a heavyweight prize fight. At least Chamberlain didn't provide Hitler with the army and funding to destroy England. On the other hand, Olmert's agreement to release prisoners and vast sums of money to Mahmoud Abbas reeks of appeasement, naivety, negligence and downright stupidity.

Some facts are worth recounting: For all the money and arms Abbas received, nothing was done to dismantle the terrorists, as required by the Road Map, especially Fatah's own Al Aksa Martyrs Brigade, which now roams Judea and Samaria to enforce Fatah's position. All weapons and armaments previously sent to bolster Abbas's credibility were, until the Gaza coup two weeks ago, used only against Israelis. At no time did Abbas make even the slightest pretense of an effort to bring a halt to the rocket fire from Gaza; this particularly before Hamas's election, i.e., during the time he and Fatah controlled the PA. Finally, Abbas has never condemned the murder of civilians for any reason other than that it does not advance the Palestinian cause; not a word that it is legally or morally wrong.

As for released prisoners agreeing to forswear terrorism, it is noteworthy that in the last five years, 179 Israelis have been murdered by terrorists who were previously in prison. Olmert is making a bad bet with the lives of his countrymen.

Olmert's vision of a two-state solution with Fatah in Judea and Samaria is worse than a mirage. Eventually a mirage disappears, but Olmert will eat sand because he doesn't know the difference – even though he may mean well.

June 13, 2007

To the Editor (IJP):

The mere suggestion that the DFLP's Nayef Hawatmeh should be permitted into Israel is a brazen statement that the lives of Israel's children are of no value and that those who kill them should be free to roam Israel's streets.

The 1974 murder of 21 schoolchildren at Ma'alot, of which Hawatmeh was the chief architect, organizer and planner, stands as one of the most infamous slaughters in the annals of Palestinian terrorism, whose murderers have shown themselves to be capable of virtually any act of inhumanity and cruelty.

To allow Hawatmeh to visit Israel under a white flag of immunity would be worse than appeasement or cowardice. It would be moral suicide. To have even allowed this inhuman creature to have lived these past 33 years is an act of unspeakable shame. Allow him into Judea and Samaria? Only to greet him with the same welcome that was accorded the murderers of Israel's athletes in Munich.

Israel and the Palestinians – What the Media Aren't Telling You

July 13, 2007

To the Editor (JReport):

Your mention of the imminent release of two Jordanians who murdered Israeli soldiers omitted one salient fact: The killers, serving life sentences in Israel, will be repatriated to Jordan where they will be jailed for only another 18 months.

Why was there no *quid pro quo* for Israel's actions? This is yet one more example of Prime Minister Olmert's inexhaustible obsequiousness and appeasement of the Arabs. Moreover, we see this same lack of a backbone in Olmert's offer to release 250 Palestinian prisoners *gratis*. At the very least, Olmert should demand the return of Gilad Shalit currently held by Hamas. Instead, we see the Palestinians pushing him around like the weak sister he is.

July 20, 2007

To the Editor (JP),

Re: "PM: Israel Should Leave West Bank, But Not Unilaterally." It's refreshing to see that PM Olmert has learned one of the lessons of Gaza, i.e., not to disengage unilaterally. On the other hand, and based on his uncanny ability to embrace mirages, I fear that the Palestinian *quid pro quo* will be to sign pledges not to commit crimes against the Israelis living inside the Green Line.

Then the question will be what is he going to do about it when the Hamas-led Palestinians break their pledge of non-violence, as they have time after time? And how will he deal with a second Hamastan in Judea and Samaria, not only armed to the teeth with all the weapons and missiles Iran and Syria can place there, but threatening to cut Israel in half by marching a mere nine miles?

Even Pavlov's dogs learned *something* from experience.

August 10, 2007

To the Editor (IJP):

Word comes to us today ("Abbas is Willing to Negotiate and Truly Seeks Peace," August 10, 2007) that PA Chairman Abbas is "a man of peace...a liberal willing to negotiate." That assessment comes not from another law-abiding member of Fatah, nor even from the Aksa Brigades, its renegade terrorists. This is not from a participant at Oslo, nor from one who stood with Sharon and Abbas at Sharm el-Sheikh. No, this assessment is from a Palestinian who lives in Syria and has the worst kind of blood on his hands – that of children. Our interlocutor's name is Nayef Hawatmeh, the head of the DFLP, and his was the mind that conceived the murder of 21 Israeli children at the schoolhouse in Ma'alot 33 years ago.

The Ma'alot murders were not your ordinary massacre where civilians die in a bomb blast or are randomly lined up against a wall and shot. No, Ma'alot was extraordinary. Hawatmeh had his men dressed up in IDF uniforms when they entered the school that day.

I wonder if they heard a sigh of relief when the children saw IDF uniforms. Did they catch that glitter in the eyes of hopeful youths as they returned to their notebooks? Did they sense the calm and security brought by those uniforms?

Were they amused at how easily they gained access to a house of study and fooled children? Did they laugh to themselves when they took out their weapons and saw the horror on the faces of those children? Did they not see the terror in those young eyes? Did they not hear the horror in those screaming young voices? Twenty-two dead, including three from the same family, and 68 more wounded. Did they do themselves and their people proud as they stepped over the bodies and slipped on the blood?

Those who committed such infamy take a back seat to the man who conceived, planned and organized the slaughter, Nayef Hawatmeh, the man whose word we are now supposed to accept that Abbas is a man of peace. By comparison, Hamas, Hizbullah,

Fatah and Islamic Jihad are amateurs. Israelis who owe the deaths of their children to Hawatmeh are not so naive as to accept from him the truth of any assertion of fact, much less an opinion of good faith and integrity.

There are some sins so egregious, so unspeakable, that they may be expiated, if at all, only in death. What Nayef Hawatmeh did at Ma'alot on May 15, 1974 is such an unredeemable sin.

Israel and the Palestinians – What the Media Aren't Telling You

August 29, 2007

Ms. Jennifer Christensen
CNN
1 CNN Center
Atlanta, GA 30303

Dear Ms. Christensen,

I remember when Ted Turner started CNN a little more than 25 years ago. Like many, I was eager to hear from a news organization that was not run by corporate conglomerates interested first in power and money and last in providing accurate, objective reporting. Over the years, however, CNN has gone the way of ABC News, the BBC and Reuters, to name a few, in its coverage of the Arab-Israeli conflict. In spite of the fact that the Palestinians, with no condemnation from CNN, specifically target Israeli civilians, it is the Israelis who are pilloried relentlessly and the Palestinians who are portrayed as innocent victims.

Sadly, Christiane Amanpour's report "God's Jewish Warriors" brutalized the Israelis and made charges that are totally unsupportable. Two stand out for reply: First was the statement by a lady that she could not be 100% American as she is also Jewish. The question of "divided loyalty" is one that the anti-Jewish community has attempted to exploit in both the United States and Europe for thousands of years. I acknowledge that there are people who feel as she does. But, the overwhelming majority of America's Jews consider themselves Americans first.

Not that our religion is irrelevant, but we know full well that we owe our first loyalties to America, a country whose freedoms are unequaled in history. For CNN to have painted with so broad a brush is a slander against Jewish Americans in general and specifically panders to those who question our loyalty solely by virtue of our religion.

Second, rather than shed light on the conflict, Ms. Amanpour pours the gasoline of misinformation on the inferno. She misleads your audience by stating, with no basis in fact, that the settlements are the primary reason the conflict continues. In support of that mendacious assertion we hear from former President Jimmy Carter, a man whose animus toward Israel is well documented and whose casual use of the incendiary word "apartheid" has been widely discredited.

Apartheid is the forceful separation of people on the basis of race. Although there are no racial differences between Israelis and Palestinians, let us for the sake of discussion bastardize the term to mean the forceful separation of people on the basis of religion or culture. On that basis, the only people who have been discriminated against are the Israelis. The litmus test was Gaza. The reason Israel had to leave was because 1.4 million Palestinians would not live in peace with 8,000 Israelis. Had that not been so, the entire subject of disengagement would never have arisen. As Gaza teaches us, this is not a boundary dispute and this is not about land. It was about making Gaza *Judenrein*. Such is the depth of their hatred.

Yet, even a *Judenrein* Gaza was not sufficient for the Palestinians. Immediately after Israel withdrew, the Palestinians destroyed not only the hi-tech greenhouses that provided Palestinian jobs, but also what was left of the synagogues. More than ridding the land of the Jews, they wanted to erase any evidence that the Jewish settlers had even been there. And then, so as to drive the point home, they fire rockets daily at Israeli cities. Indeed, cities which are within pre-1967 Israel. (Curiously, Ms. Amanpour is apparently not troubled by this.) That should eloquently tell us what lies ahead should Israel abandon Judea and Samaria. No settlements. No Jews. Continued terrorism.

You have to ask yourself what the real reason is that the settlements are even an issue. It is not sufficient to urge as the Palestinians do, that it is "our land." Putting the dubiousness of that claim aside, does that mean that nobody else can live there? The Palestinians answer in the affirmative. Yes, that is exactly what it means.

It is worth recalling that the West introduced troops into

Central Europe when ethnic cleansing took so many lives. Even in pre-1991 South Africa, blacks may have been segregated, but they were still allowed to live in the country, albeit under horrible circumstances. Yet the Palestinians want "their land" to be more apartheid than South Africa was – the Jews can't even live there. Thus, the settlements are an issue because the Palestinians want even Judea and Samaria, the historical center of Judaism, also to be *Judenrein*. CNN's silence on this matter is most damning and bespeaks its own pernicious prejudice.

As for Mr. Carter's "apartheid" Israel, over a million Arabs live there with full Israeli citizenship. Israeli Arabs have the rights of all Israelis, for example, to own land and vote. There are Arab Israelis in the Knesset and an Arab Israeli minister in Israel's cabinet. Why was Mr. Carter not confronted with those facts? The charge of apartheid is a lie, yet CNN abandoned journalistic ethics and led its viewers into a sewage of prejudice with only the veiled pretense of fairness.

Where were CNN's and Ms. Amanpour's sharp tongues when Israeli women and children were being blown up by jihadist Palestinians who declared that, rather than raise their children, they would rather "knock at the door to paradise holding the skulls of the Zionists"?

I have to conclude that CNN is stuck in the mud of bias, and that CNN treats its obligation for objectivity as merely a word for journalism students. As matters presently stand, CNN's credibility is on a life-support system. To paraphrase the late Adlai Stevenson, credibility is to a journalist what virtue is to a lady. You must decide what you are and what you are going to do about it.

cc: Ms. Christiane Amanpour
   Mr. James Walton (Pres., CNN News)

September 23, 2007

To the Editor (NYTimes):

My father taught me many things when I was growing up. One in particular comes to mind at this time. When I was 13 years old he sensed that something was wrong. "What's on your mind, son?" "Nothing," I said softly as I averted his gaze. "Well," he said, "as long as you're OK, that's fine. But listen to me for a second. You can fool your teachers and maybe even your mother and me. But don't try to fool yourself. You can't do it without it damaging your soul." He was, of course, right, and whenever I tried to persuade myself that something was other than it really was, it would jump up and bite me on the ass.

Self-delusion rears its ugly head again tomorrow when Iran's President Ahmadinejad visits New York. He will address the United Nations, as is well his right as the leader of a member nation. Following his address, however, he will address students and faculty at Columbia University.

Two reasons to meet with Ahmadinejad come to mind. The first is out of curiosity. An opportunity to observe him much in the way a physician examines a cancerous cell under a microscope. "What form of matter is before us and how does it behave?" they might ask out of scientific methodology. Poke it. Push it. How does it respond to stimulus?

The second reason is to converse with and question him, which I admit is the more likely reason – although I believe we can learn more about this gangster in a biology lab. What do they think he can possibly say to sanitize statements such as "Israel must be wiped off the map," "the Holocaust is a myth," and that he believes that in a nuclear exchange 50% is an acceptable price for his fellow Iranians to pay for the destruction of Israel? Will they break bread with a man who yearns for nuclear holocaust, Armageddon, so an Islamic caliphate may rule what is left of the world?

Israel and the Palestinians – What the Media Aren't Telling You

I suppose one day Columbia President Lee Bollinger, who issued the invitation, can bounce his grandchildren on his knees and tell them of the time they met and exchanged ideas with the single most dangerous person to live since Adolph Hitler. Whether it's a nice bedtime story, or simply grotesque hubris, it won't provide an answer to the question, "But Grandpa, what did you do to stop him from doing all the terrible things he told you he was going to do?"

What do they think they can learn at Ahmadinejad's knee? Do they really think he will tell America why Israel must be destroyed? Why America must be destroyed? Why Iran is sending soldiers and armaments into Iraq to kill American soldiers? Will they believe him when he tells them, as he surely will, that Iran's nuclear intentions are peaceful? Knowing in advance that he will lie to us, what purpose is served by his presence?

I fully expect Columbia's trustees and faculty will proclaim that "freedom of speech" and "academic freedom" are alive and robust at Columbia. But that is just smoke. This is not about the exchange of competing ideas that can withstand intellectual scrutiny. This is about character and judgment. It is about values. Next week, the students of Columbia should debate, not Ahmadinejad's disingenuous mendacity, but rather, why they invited the most dangerous man in the world into their home.

The concept of academic freedom was shredded when John Coatsworth, dean of Columbia's School of Public and International Affairs, conceded that he would have invited Hitler to Columbia. *Reductio ad absurdum* – if one man can instruct us, then any man may instruct us. Churchill well and truly understood that Hitler posed an existential threat to Great Britain, and it was only for that reason that he allied himself with the only slightly less demented Joseph Stalin. To save Europe, he reckoned, he would dine with the devil and worry about it later, if they were still alive.

As the Pooh-Bahs of America's media and Ivy League nod heads, or cluck their thick tongues, Ahmadinejad will laugh all the way home to Teheran.

What are the leaders of one of our most prestigious universities doing in bed with a man who would kill us all instantly if he only had the means? Do they think they can do business with this Iranian creature?

As my father would have asked, "Who do you think you're kidding?"

Israel and the Palestinians – What the Media Aren't Telling You

October 9, 2007

To the Editor (Newsday):

Re: Olmert denies Jerusalem partition talk (10/9/07): If Israeli PM Olmert really believes that partition of Jerusalem, inter alia, will bring peace to Israel, then he has become a victim of his own hubris and obsequiousness. No nation on Earth would consider yielding the embodiment of its soul. For to do so would be seen to substantiate the Palestinian claim that Israel has no historical right to any part of Jerusalem, as was intoned by Mr. Arafat to President Clinton at Camp David in 2000. Israel without Jerusalem would be Israel without the Divine spark.

It is irrelevant that the Palestinians ask for only half of Jerusalem, inasmuch as Jewish rights, cemeteries and holy places have never been respected under anyone else's jurisdiction. Jerusalem cannot exist one-half Jewish and one-half apartheid.

What is also likely is that the Palestinian plan for the staged destruction of Israel – verified time and again by the "moderate" Abbas – will begin with the staged annexation of Jerusalem.

Gaza provides us with valuable insight into what awaits a dejudaized Jerusalem: expulsion of all Jews; destruction of all Jewish synagogues; the removal of all evidence that Jews have *ever* lived there. It has already started on the Temple Mount – the most sacred site in Judaism – with the destruction of artifacts dating back thousands of years.

As a righteous man is reputed to have told Mephistopheles, "You may take my body, and you may even cut out my heart, but you can never have my soul."

For the Record

October 15, 2007

Mr. Steve Kroft
60 Minutes
524 West 57th St.
New York, New York 10019

Re: Dubai

Dear Mr. Kroft,

I found your interview last night with Dubai's ruler, Sheikh Muhammad bin Rashid al Maktoum, to be particularly informative. As one in the construction industry, I was truly impressed by how much has been accomplished there, albeit with the backing and participation of his government.

There is, however, one problem in this Arabian utopia which you seem to have avoided – a pervasive anti-Israel prejudice. Curiously, you failed to press the matter when Sheikh Maktoum told you that he wanted the United States to change "one element" of its foreign relations. What I find troublesome is that a journalist of your reputation obsequiously let the sheikh off the hook by refusing to ask him to identify the "problem" nation. This one incident turned your "investigative story" into a commercial for Dubai. Sadly, this was reminiscent of Mike Wallace's softball interview with Iranian President Ahmadinejad.

It was reported today that Dubai has refused entry visas to Israelis for next week's World Congress of the FIATA, the International Federation of Freight Forwarders Association. (FIATA is an NGO which represents an industry covering approximately 40,000 forwarding and logistics firms, employing 8–10 million people in 150 countries.)

Furthermore, it is noteworthy that Dubai has joined the Arab boycott and is actively enforcing a trade embargo against Israel.

You may also find it of interest that a couple of years ago, the Emirates purchased sophisticated medical equipment from the Israelis – equipment which was returned because they were marked as having been made in Israel. So much for Sheikh Maktoum's humanitarian concern for his people.

This information would have given your viewers a clearer understanding of a country portrayed on 60 Minutes as a veritable Garden of Eden worthy of emulation. Perhaps you will do a 15 or 20 second follow-up to the story on the next 60 Minutes.

For the Record

November 7, 2007

To the Editor (NYT):

Your article "Gaza's Reflection in a Foul Threat" (11/7/07) properly describes the disgusting situation caused by the sea of sewage overtaking Gazan communities. Yet, it is relevant to understand the context: that it was revealed back in March 2007, when the situation first presented, that Israel had provided drainage pipes to the Palestinians (then under the control of Fatah leader Mahmoud Abbas) that would have brought modernity to their sewerage system.

Instead of using the Israeli pipe for health infrastructure, the Palestinians used the pipe to construct launching platforms and Kassam rockets to fire into pre-1967 Israel, specifically at Sderot.

The Palestinians have received more foreign aid per capita than any other nation on earth. In fact, less money was spent on the Marshall Plan. Instead of using such international largesse to improve their lives, the Palestinians have used these resources to kill Israelis.

Israel and the Palestinians – What the Media Aren't Telling You

November 26, 2007

To the Editor (NYT):

Roger Cohen's Op-Ed ("Bush's Best Hope" 11/26/07) misses the mark on four critical points. First, contrary to his characterization, the PA is not a combination of Tammany Hall and the Keystone Cops. Whatever ineptitude they suffer flows from their inability to sell themselves and their ideas to their people.

Second, a return to the notorious "Holocaust lines" is a prescription for terror, not peace. There can be no doubt that without the IDF, the West Bank would come under the Islamic iron fist of Hamas and, by extension, Iran and Syria. Gaza stands as eloquent proof.

Third, by urging a freeze of all West Bank settlements, even insofar as is necessary for natural growth, Mr. Cohen takes the first step toward the ethnic cleansing of Jews from the West Bank and the establishment of apartheid there, again mirroring the experience of Gaza.

Fourth, conspicuously absent from Mr. Cohen's equation for peace is the end of terrorism.

Mr. Fayyad, in whom Mr. Cohen reposes so much trust, says, "In 1993 we renounced violence…" Would that it were so.

For the Record

November 28, 2007

To the Editor (IJP):

News today that Cardinal Renato Martino, a Vatican official, urged a "right of return" for the Palestinians ("Vatican Official backs Right of Return" 11/28/07) is a staggering blow to Jewish-Catholic relations. It is beyond peradventure that this Vatican official is well aware of the fact that a Palestinian "right of return" will extinguish Israel's identity – her *raison d'être* – as a Jewish state.

Moreover, given the import of this monstrously anti-Semitic statement, one may well assume that it was first cleared by the pope, himself a former soldier of the Third Reich. Whatever misgivings world Jewry had when Cardinal Ratzinger became Pope Benedict XVI became galvanized today.

What the Vatican was doing getting itself in the middle of the Israeli-Palestinian conflict is hard enough to explain, but for it to have taken sides against its elder, historical and theological cognate is as a knife in the back.

What does it mean when the Vatican urges the destruction of the world's only Jewish state? It is, first and foremost, a breathtaking declaration of anti-Semitism. More than that, it tells the world's Catholics that anti-Semitism is acceptable, i.e., no longer *verboten*. Second, it encourages acts of anti-Semitism not only among Catholics, but also throughout Europe, and anywhere else his word is *ex cathedra*, or even slightly authoritative. Third, it is evidence to the world's Muslims that Jews are the illegitimate occupiers of all of Israel, and not just the West Bank.

The pope may issue all the ecumenical declarations his heart desires, but, as Lady Macbeth found out, this is one stain that won't wash out.

Israel and the Palestinians – What the Media Aren't Telling You

November 27, 2007

To the Editor (Newsday):
Re: "LI Pols mixed on Mideast Talk" (11/27/07)

The suggestion that removal of all Israeli settlements in Judea and Samaria is necessary for peace, while having the grace of convenience is, side by side with the demand for a Palestinian "right of return," the most pernicious of the proposed solutions. Its attraction is its simplicity, but the reality behind that illusion is the ethnic cleansing of Jews from their ancient homeland strictly on the basis of their religion. That is, after all, the operative definition of apartheid: the forced separation of a people on the basis of race or religion.

America has dealt with this nasty sort of thing before, in the early days of racial integration. James Meredith, the Kennedy administration decided, was going to enroll in the University of Mississippi because it was his right. JFK called in the army, federal marshals and National Guard to put down the riots and Meredith was enrolled at "Ole Miss." Violence would not be permitted to trump the Constitution. Peace would not be purchased with the rights of the minority.

What I cannot abide is that America now stands mute knowing full well that the Palestinians unashamedly demand the expulsion of all Jews from *their* homeland. By what perversion of ethics and morality is President Bush prepared to accede to the application of apartheid against Israel's Jews, particularly after the example that was set in South Africa? How do you suppose the Palestinians would react if Israel, in response to this Palestinian demand to make Judea and Samaria *Judenrein*, demanded the expulsion of all Palestinians from Israel? Sauce for the goose?

The expulsion of Israel's Jews – Israel's Arabs are not subject to this cleansing, and that is why it is not just anti-Israeli, but also anti-Semitic – is necessary because the Palestinians refuse to tolerate the presence of *any* Jews. That was the lesson of Gaza: 1.4 million Palestinians refused to live in peace with 8,000 Jews, and from the "civilized" West we heard not so much as a muffled objection. Peace in Gaza, such as it is, was treated like a mathematical equation, utterly devoid of concepts of right and wrong. Only a sense of suicide demands that Israel repeat the crime in Judea and Samaria. The solution to the "settlers" is tolerance, not apartheid.

Of course, even the removal of the Jewish settlers from Judea and Samaria will not bring peace, any more than it did in Gaza. In fact, the dejudaization of Judea and Samaria, and withdrawal of the IDF, will be, with almost metaphysical certitude, but a prelude to a Hamas takeover there and the progression of Iranian hegemony.

What kind of peace is achieved if its linchpin is apartheid? Is that the nature of America's foreign policy? Let us at least be honest about what the settlers represent and what their expulsion really signifies. It is nothing less than the same anti-Semitism that has haunted the Middle East for over 3,000 years. But now, with America and Europe as the prime facilitators, it is not merely a regional hatred. In every sense of the word, those who acquiesce in the removal of the settlers – particularly the United States and Europe – are aiders and abettors. Their silence does more than signify consent and it is worse than appeasement. It is participation.

Israel and the Palestinians – What the Media Aren't Telling You

December 19, 2007

To the Editor (NYT):

Your editorial "Down Payment for Peace" (12/19/07) makes the mistake of thinking money is the cure for all evils. The international community's pledge of $7.4 billion would be inspiring if we didn't know it was so futile. The European and American donors make the decades-old mistake of believing that peace with one's enemy is a commodity that can be purchased like bread in a bakery. The Palestinians have had more money per capita thrown at them than any people in history. More than was even given under the Marshall Plan.

The problem is what the Palestinian leaders have done with that money: billions stolen outright; palatial villas and expensive cars for the favored few; bribes; virulent, non-stop incitement in government-controlled schools and media, not to mention mosques; and terrorist training camps and weaponry.

PA Prime Minister Fayyad has already conceded that the vast majority of the funds will be used to pay salaries of the bloated PA security forces. Only the naive would believe that even a single refugee camp will be demolished and replaced with suitable housing. It is doubtful that any money will be used to make the lives of the Palestinians any better. And that serves the interests of the PA's leaders just fine, since unemployment and hunger well and truly fuel anger and hatred. It is easier to inspire hatred than hope, and these leaders would rather point the finger at Israel and America than look in the mirror.

Neither is diplomacy, as you urge, going to resolve the enmity; it has been tried unsuccessfully by the Israelis numerous times. The Palestinians want every single Jew out of Judea and Samaria; and then they will want every Jew out of Israel. That is, and has been, their true intent. You can't make peace with an enemy who has his heart set on your annihilation.

This conflict will continue for many more generations until God issues the one commandment He overlooked: Thou shalt not hate.

For the Record

December 20, 2007

To the Editor (JP):

Michael Felsen's essay ("Speaking Truth for Peace," December 19, 2007) urging Israel to tell the truth about not having been a godsend to the Palestinians is all well and good, but it lacks context.

Has the IDF been deployed to Judea and Samaria? Yes, but the question is why? Like so many of the other restrictions imposed on the Palestinians, it was necessary to prevent Palestinian terrorism and to protect all lives in Israel, Jewish and Arab.

Israel's protective devices pale in comparison to the horrors undertaken by the PA: suicide bombers, explosive devices on roads, firing of rockets and mortars at civilians, and the inculcation of blind hatred through its media and education system.

When the Palestinians own up to, renounce and cease their treachery, then let Mr. Felsen talk about Israel's modest shortcomings.

January 30, 2008

To the Editor (JP):

When we were toddlers, our mothers had to warn us not to touch the hot stove. For most, this was a lesson easily learned, and a painful mistake not repeated.

Sheldon Schreter's essay "For the cause, the settlements must go" (29 January 2008) made me both sad and frustrated. I fear for a two-state future on a number of levels, but the question that must be asked is why the dejudaization of Judea and Samaria is a condition for peace.

If the disengagement from Gaza was wrong, it was wrong for more reasons than because Gaza predictably became a terrorist entity. The Palestinian demand that every last one of the settlers be removed – backed by Israeli, American and European complicity – was blatant anti-Semitism. Do you think that if native American Indians suddenly rioted, demanding independence and the expulsion of all non-Indians from South Dakota, that the United States would take the demand seriously, much less agree?

The daily barrage of rockets and mortars showed that the true equation was land without peace.

Now history is looking to repeat itself in Judea and Samaria, the cradle of the Jewish people and the most historically significant land of our existence. And once again we are asked to believe that this expulsion – the last territorial demand of the Arabs? – from our biblical heritage will bring us that very peace and acceptance for which we have waited in vain since our first expulsion.

Messrs. Bush and Olmert, arm in arm with Mesdames Rice and Livni, again stand behind Israel at the precipice urging us forward yet again. The Palestinians have already told us that they will not tolerate any Jews in "their" homeland. In fact, only last month, a PA spokesman assured us that they would not lift a finger to protect any Jews remaining in Judea and Samaria.

And, the Americans and Europeans are standing there prepared to lead us out of the promised land.

Why has no one questioned the ethic or morality of

demanding that Judea and Samaria be *Judenrein*? We'll hear no to hear objections from *The New York Times*, CNN, the BBC or Reuters. But where are the voices of the Israelis? Why would the editor of *Ha'aretz*, rather than see his country flourish, ask the American secretary of state to have it "raped"? Why do the leaders of the Likud, Yisrael Beiteinu or Shas not demand an explanation for why Jews cannot live in peace in a Palestinian state – or anywhere else, for that matter? Mr. Schreter is in pain over the "rightness" of Israel's conduct, but fails to explain why religious cleansing is right.

One may ask whether the Israelis should expel all Arabs from Israel so long as they insist on expelling all Jews from Judea and Samaria. Sauce for the goose, perhaps? The demand to remove the settlers is conclusive evidence that this conflict is not about borders. It is not about Palestinian autonomy. It is not about Palestinian nationalism. It is about Jews. Until that reality is accepted, no peace conference can resolve this conflict.

Nor is this about what Mr. Schreter calls "pragmatic Zionism." It is true that Ben Gurion decided that half a loaf was better than none, but this is not about creating borders and carving up land. It is the principle of *Judenrein*, which has caused us to be a people without a land for millennia; a principle that dictates that Jews – wherever we may be – guests in someone else's home. Pragmatism will take us only so far.

Mr. Schreter also decries the loss of the "essential rightness of our cause." I believe he is referring to our right to live in peace. But the right to live in peace does not mean live in peace only in Israel. Why should Jews not be allowed to live in peace in Palestine? In Saudi Arabia? In Syria? In Lebanon and Jordan? That, too, is the "rightness of our cause."

If, as Mr. Schreter opines, "the most important proof in the arsenal of our enemies is precisely the settlements," then they must be compelled to explain why the mere presence of Jews so toxic.

I find it curious that Mr. Schreter concurs with our enemies

Israel and the Palestinians – What the Media Aren't Telling You

that the security fence is a land grab. Is it of no significance that the fence saves lives by impeding terrorists? Moreover, the barrier can, and in the past has been, moved to accommodate genuine Palestinian concerns while maintaining its protective function. (Did Mr. Schreter object to the Egyptian wall at its border with Gaza, which Hamas just destroyed?)

Mr. Schreter asks us to be content with the pre-1967 Israel. I wish to point out that the rockets and mortars being fired daily at Sderot and Ashkelon *are* hitting inside pre-1967 Israel. The armistice borders are not sacrosanct.

Mr. Schreter is correct that "withdrawing from the settlements will not appease our enemies, nor should we leave unilaterally, without guarantees, safeguards and milestones." The problem is that there are no guarantees or promises which the Palestinians can make that are credible. They have lied their way past the Israelis ever since Oslo. They have failed to make any substantive effort to live in peace. To this very day, the official Palestinian media, which remain controlled by Abbas, continue to spew anti-Israel and anti-Semitic incitement. One after another, Palestinian promises lie next to each other rotting in the gutter. That Olmert actually believes that Abbas is a man of peace is tragic.

And Gaza has taught us another lesson: appeasement does not work. It is a sign of weakness in the Arab world, to be met with increased hostility and violence. Olmert could offer Abbas *all* of Israel except the Tel Aviv Hilton and that would still not suffice. The Middle East is a venue of ongoing war with only interstitial moments of calm.

Surely, Mr. Schreter understands that the IDF's presence in Judea and Samaria is the only thing standing between Abbas and a Hamas takeover of what is left of the PA. If the IDF pulls out of Judea and Samaria, Hamas will take control there quicker than you can say Aldo Moro.

The Palestinians continue to take all and give nothing. They get prisoners, money, electricity, fuel, checkpoints closed, and road blocks lifted; while Israel gets only continued incitement and terrorism. Like a dysfunctional 3-year-old, she keeps putting her hand on the hot stove in efforts to prop up Abbas and the PA.

If 3,000 years of wars, pogroms and expulsions, and particularly what has transpired in Gaza, are not adequate reasons not to continue to appease the Palestinians then Olmert is incapable and unfit to lead Israel.

February 4, 2008

To the Editor (JP):

Defense Minister Barak says that the terrorist attack in Dimona ("Barak: Attack Justifies Staying in Government" 4 Feb. 2008) shows why he must remain in the government. In fact, Mr. Barak has it backwards. It is precisely because of the suicide bombing in Dimona – Israel's most security sensitive location – that he must resign from Olmert's government. And this after the area was placed on a high alert following the breach of the Gaza-Egypt border.

The Olmert government's failure – yes, another significant failure – to prevent terrorism in Dimona requires the prime minister's removal inasmuch as he does not have the honor or integrity to resign.

How many examples are necessary to drive home the point that PM Olmert has not the slightest clue about how to defend Israel and her citizens? The Gaza disengagement, the Second Lebanese War, the daily terrorism against Sderot, the Hamas takeover of Gaza, etc. The list goes on.

Anyone who remains in this government is, certainly at this point, guilty of complicity and deserves to be painted with the same brush as marks the prime minister.

February 18, 2008

To the Editor (NYT):

As much as I concur with Ronen Bergman (Op-Ed "Bracing for Revenge" February 18, 2008) about the anxiety of waiting for Hizbullah's bloody reply to the assassination of its master terrorist, Imad Mugniyah, he doesn't suggest an alternative to targeted killings of the terrorist leaders. It may well be that there is none.

Yes, it is very likely that Israel will suffer civilian casualties, but if Mugniyah had been killed 30 years ago, there are hundreds of US Marines and scores of civilians who would likely be alive today. The terrorists have made this a fight to the death. We have not been given a choice and must, therefore, make the preservation of our lives paramount.

When you are being hunted – as are Americans and Israelis, by Arab terrorists – one does not have the luxury of rational debate. And if self-preservation is an instinct we possess, then self-defense is a right we must exercise.

Israel and the Palestinians – What the Media Aren't Telling You

March 7, 2008

To the Editor (NYT):

Your story on the slaughter of eight students in a Jerusalem yeshiva referred to the killer as a "gunman." Why did you not call the murderer what he was: a terrorist? This cold-hearted terrorist entered a school of religious study with a handgun and an AK-47. He had enough ammunition that during the massacre he was able to stop and reload several times.

The refusal of the *Times* to characterize Arab murderers as terrorists is strong evidence of its prejudice in this war. You characterized the men who flew the planes on 9/11 as terrorists. Why is this different? Is it that Americans are murdered by terrorists and Israelis by gunmen?

Moreover, you didn't hesitate to report that a few of the Israelis gathered at the yeshiva called for "Death to the Arabs." But, you didn't report that the Gazans celebrated this massacre at a religious school by shooting guns into the air and handing out candy. Why did you withhold those facts from your readers?

APPENDIX OF ESSAYS

Self-Defense – Both a Sword and a Shield

For the first time in history, the fundamental right of a nation to defend itself from aggression has been seriously called into question, and it is no coincidence that the victim of this malevolent cynicism is the State of Israel.

Beirut is now totally encircled by the Israel Defense Forces. Thousands of civilians, both Lebanese and Palestinian, have left the PLO just where they belong – on their own. The offices, homes and schools of Beirut are empty and the PLO is like a kidnapper without a hostage. Israel has offered to let the PLO leave Lebanon with their lives and, remarkably, their weapons. If anyone thinks the PLO would have exhibited the same quality of mercy, let them read the chapter of Israel's history under "Ma'alot."

Yet, Israel has been roundly and ferociously criticized, as though PLO intransigence, terrorism and murder were a fair price to pay for Western and Egyptian recognition of Israel's right to exist. The singularly dangerous implication of such criticism is that any nation – particularly Israel, alone among nations – should be denied the fundamental right to defend her citizens and borders.

In 1859, John Stuart Mill wrote: "The sole end for which

For the Record

mankind are warranted, individually or collectively, in interfering with the liberty of action of any of their number is self-protection." Until June 6, 1982, this principle was universally accepted and stood as an admonishment against military aggression. Now, however, insofar as Israel is concerned, the right of self-defense has become less a matter of principle than of whose ox is gored.

Ever since the Palestinians and the PLO were driven out of Jordan in 1970, not only has the game changed but so have the rules. The name of the game has been terrorism, with different rules applicable to each side. For the PLO, which is constitutionally dedicated to Israel's destruction, a fact which is often conveniently overlooked, the only rule was that there were no rules. For the Israelis, the first rule was to turn the other cheek; the second rule was to respect international borders; and, the third rule was to obey the other two rules, particularly the first.

The PLO, shielded by Lebanese and Palestinian civilians, has become the Arab states' battlefield proxy and Israel has been required to reinvent the wheel to justify the defense of her own citizens and borders.

When Lebanon, in no small measure due to PLO dissemblers, became completely unhinged by a civil war that ravaged its social, political and religious fabric, the PLO became the primary beneficiary of that turmoil and chaos. Before the UN disgraced itself by labeling Zionism a form of racism, the PLO had shamelessly sponsored the massacre of Israeli athletes at the 1972 Munich Olympics; the savage murder of tourists and other civilians on the beaches of Tel Aviv, the Tel Aviv-Haifa coastal road, open air markets and bus terminals in Jerusalem, and the schoolhouse at Ma'alot. Recently, in the midst of a "cease-fire," the PLO continued to bomb Israeli towns in the Galilee while the Syrians maintained sophisticated offensive weapons in Lebanon's Beka'a Valley, only miles from Israel's border.

By what right, we are asked, has Israel attacked Tyre, Sidon and western Beirut. By what right did the Israel Air Force destroy or immobilize the entire Syrian battery of Soviet-made SAM missile sites in the Beka'a Valley? The answers are indeed quite simple. It's just that the questions themselves have been riddled with assumptions – based on the "rules of the game" – that cannot withstand the scrutiny of intellectual honesty. The answers, of course, lie in the right of any nation to defend itself irrespective of international borders – a right now denied to Israel by the Arabs and the United Nations, which gave political legitimization to the Ma'alot murderers.

Grotius wrote in 1625 in *The Law of War and Peace* that self-defense is "the first just cause of war [and] this right of self-defense derives its origin primarily from the instinct of self-preservation, which nature has given to every creature.... Every man by nature is a defender of his own rights..."

Criticism for the death of Lebanese civilians, surely tragic, is nonetheless conveniently and typically misdirected at the Israelis. The responsibility, however, must be laid at the doorstep of the PLO and the Lebanese government. When the PLO callously shielded itself and stored its weapons in Lebanese homes, offices and schools, it effectively held the people of Lebanon hostage against Israeli retaliation. The Lebanese government, by its refusal or inability to disassociate itself from, and control, terrorists operating within its borders, lent the unmistakable imprimatur of its consent to the PLO and its modus operandi.

As long as the PLO was permitted to hide safely in civilian centers, behind the skirt of the Lebanese border, the probability of and necessity for an Israeli incursion inevitably increased. Under the circumstances, the response of the Begin government was necessary, proper and predictable. Just as the first right of a nation is to defend itself, the first obligation of a government is to protect the lives of its citizens. Had Israel not already made it clear at Entebbe, Tel Aviv and Ma'alot that the terrorists themselves will face swift and deadly retribution? Only, the PLO and the Syrians, emboldened by their own misguided self-importance, Soviet military support, Arab propaganda, and a Western foreign policy consistently measured by the price of oil, were foolish enough to believe that Begin and Sharon would permit the status quo to continue. As the PLO, behind a shield of flesh and blood, terrorized and killed Israelis, the world stood silent.

The linchpin of Middle East peace, we are told, is not the cessation of Arab hostility and PLO terrorism, but rather Israel's agreement to return to its pre-1967 borders, the creation of a Palestinian state on the West Bank, the dismemberment of Jerusalem and the cessation of Israeli "aggression." History itself puts the lie to the Arab line and even Israel's destruction would not bring peace to the Middle East. Internecine warfare is no stranger to the Arabs. Witness the Iran-Iraq War, Iran's own national reign of terror, Iraq's use of poison gas on her own citizens, Jordan's murder and expulsion of the Palestinians in 1970, Syria's massacre of Palestinians at Hama and de facto annexation of southern Lebanon, and Arafat's response to the assassination of Sadat ("We shake the hand that fired the gun!"). Indeed, the Arabs are themselves so steeped in blood that, as Isaiah said, sin has piled on sin.

In the aftermath of Secretary of State Haig's resignation, many Jewish Americans – who chanced a Reagan White House on the strength of candidate Reagan's strong pro-Israel platform – are expressing grave concern over the emerging influence of America's Bechtel-Saudi secretary of defense. The Arabs may refuse to deal with Israel on the diplomatic level, but unless they reconcile themselves to Israel's right to exist, political Darwinism requires Israel to take matters in a hostile world into her own hands.

The "inexhaustible obsequiousness," as George Will so aptly put it, of the Western nations to the Arab blackmailers and terrorists cannot destroy the inexhaustible courage and tenacity of Israel and the Jewish people. Neither the slavery imposed by the Pharaohs, the Roman assault on Masada, the destruction of the Temple by the Babylonians and Romans, the Spanish Inquisition, the concentration camps and gas chambers of Nazi Germany, nor the combined assaults of all the Arab armies four times in a generation could break our spirit. What kind of people do they think we are that we would crumble beneath the weight of a barrel of oil?

July 14, 1982

For the Record

Hafez Letter to The New York Times

On February 18, 1986, The New York Times published a particularly long letter from the Egyptian Embassy in Washington, highly critical of Israel in failing to promote better relations with Egypt.

To the Editor (NYT):

The February 18, 1986 letter of Abdallah Fouad Hafez (minister counselor for the Press and Information Bureau of the Egyptian Embassy in Washington) misrepresents Egypt's role in "normalizing" Israeli-Egyptian relations. Egypt, Mr. Hafez opines, has acted responsibly to normalize relations – which can now be best described as a bitter cold peace – but ignores facts, relying instead on half-truths and outright falsehoods. "To set the record straight," he points to a number of issues, none of which, I suggest, can withstand scrutiny.

First, Mr. Hafez states that once negotiations with Israel are complete "on how to put the issue of the Taba beach on the Gulf of Aqaba to arbitration" then "there is nothing to prevent our ambassador from going back to his post in Israel." Mr. Hafez's point is convenient but not persuasive. Egypt recalled its ambassador from Israel to protest Israel's incursion into Lebanon in 1982. Israel is out of Lebanon, and Egypt's ambassador is still in Egypt. Last year Lebanon was the excuse and this year it is Taba. What will it be next year now that Israel has agreed to arbitrate the Taba issue? Thus, I am compelled to conclude that Egypt has withheld the resumption of diplomatic ties with Israel without good cause, thereby placing its bona fides in serious doubt.

Second, to evidence the normalization of trade and tourism, Mr. Hafez says that more than 200,000 Israelis have traveled to Egypt and that Egypt sells to Israel more than $600 million of oil a year. But that is what Egypt got from Israel. What did Israel get from Egypt under the "normalization?" How many Egyptians gave a boost to Israel's economy through tourism? At what price did Egypt sell to Israel the oil from the Sinai fields, which Israel

Israel and the Palestinians – What the Media Aren't Telling You

discovered and developed? What quid pro quo did Israel receive for bolstering a bankrupt Egyptian economy? Answers to any of these questions are conspicuously absent and strongly suggest that Egypt has taken much and given little, if anything, in return.

Third, Mr. Hafez cites Ezer Weizman's recent trip to Cairo as evidence that the two countries "have exchanged numerous ministerial visits." What is not disclosed by Mr. Hafez is the cold shoulder Minister Weizman received from President Mubarak. Camp David does not talk in terms of an exchange of visits on the "ministerial level." It speaks of the exchange of ambassadors. Nevertheless, Mr. Hafez does not cite to us any example of an Egyptian minister having gone to Israel on any substantive matter.

Fourth, the Ras Burka incident – in which an Egyptian policeman slaughtered seven Israeli tourists, four of them children – is lightly dismissed as "an isolated and individual act that could happen anywhere in the world." Yet, Mr. Hafez fails to explain the fact that the government-controlled media lionized this murderer and thus incited the Egyptian people to declare the miscreant to be a hero and the seven dead Israelis as deserving so brutal a fate. No mention was made of Egypt's manipulation of its citizenry. Disingenuously, we are told that "Egypt has offered to Israeli authorities a 25-page court document," but we are not told why that document has yet to be delivered or what it says.

Fifth, Mr. Hafez praises "Egypt's relentless efforts to keep the peace process going," which, he says, have encouraged "the moderate elements in the Palestinian camp." There are moderates in the Palestinian camp? Within the last six months, President Mubarak has hosted PLO Chairman Arafat a number of times. And each time, Arafat – strutting shoulder to shoulder with Egypt's president – has tossed one grenade after another at the peace process which Mr. Hafez claims his government holds so dear. Witness, for example, Arafat's "Cairo Declaration." After Jordan's King Hussein urged Arafat to recognize Israel, denounce the *Achille Lauro* fiasco and engage in a constructive peace dialogue, Arafat spit in his face, flew to Cairo, met the press with President Mubarak, and stated that the Palestinian people should resist by any means Israel's occupation of any part of Palestine, which he considers to be all of Israel.

If Mr. Hafez is to be believed about Egypt's "relentless efforts to keep the peace process going, to enlarge its circle and to encourage the moderate elements in the Palestinian camp," then President Mubarak's conduct is bizarre and inexplicable.

Most notable perhaps are the factual liberties which Mr. Hafez takes with regard to the PLO. Egypt takes credit for the February 11, 1986 "agreement" between Jordan and the PLO. That "agreement" had a remarkably short life. Only one month later, King Hussein sought to maroon Arafat and to enlist so-called moderate Palestinian Arabs. (Hussein's efforts, however, probably died with the assassination of Zafer al-Masri, mayor of Nablus.) Nevertheless, Egypt's motive in designing a Jordanian-PLO rapprochement was ostensibly to seduce Jordan away from the Syrian camp and to shore up Arafat, Mubarak's own battlefield proxy.

But this is almost kid stuff. Mr. Hafez joins the major leagues by stating, with a straight face, that "the PLO accepted...all United Nations resolutions, a peaceable solution to the conflict and a confederation with Jordan." The PLO has never accepted United Nations Resolutions 242 and 338. The PLO is less inclined to share the West Bank with Jordan than Egypt is to return the Sinai to Israel. Mr. Hafez is no less disingenuous in invoking the Cairo Declaration – for which Egypt claims credit, perhaps properly – and asserting that it "condemned acts of terrorism against civilians anywhere." The Cairo Declaration did no such thing. To the contrary, it expressly acknowledged that the "armed struggle" against all people – neither women nor children being excluded – within "occupied" Palestine, i.e. Israel, would continue.

Insofar as Mr. Hafez proclaims the right of "the Palestinian people" to self-determination, "a basic tenet of American heritage," it is revealing that he fails to acknowledge that the Palestinian Arabs of Gaza, Judea and Samaria have been afforded their own state time and again, but have chosen war rather than coexist with a Jewish state. Nevertheless, they enjoy greater freedom and a higher standard of living than the people of Jordan, Egypt, Syria or Lebanon. The Palestinian Arabs who left Israel in 1948 did so at the urging of the Arabs who promised them they could return to a *Judenrein* Palestine to reclaim not only their homes, but those of the soon-to-be-dead Jews. Mr. Hafez conveniently overlooks the fact that the partition of Palestine made land west of the Jordan River part of the Jewish state, which Jordan occupied for 19 years before Israel liberated it and two-thirds of Jerusalem in the Six Day War. Under Jordanian rule, the Palestinian Arabs were denied Jordanian citizenship or, in Mr. Hafez's terms, the right of self-determination. And what has Egypt done since 1948 to ameliorate the situation? Four times in 24 years it waged war against Israel, leaving the Palestinian Arabs, whom it claims to hold so dear, in the crossfire.

I believe Mr. Hafez to be well aware of the truth. His statements, however, do not square with the facts and are indeed truly representative of the Egyptian tenets that there must never be an official Jewish presence in the Middle East and that Zionism in philosophy, much less in reality, is hateful and blasphemous. It is unlikely that the cold peace between Egypt and Israel will thaw under President Mubarak's leadership or Mr. Hafez's convenient rewriting of history.

February 20, 1986

For the Record

The Middle East "Peace" Conference

Once again the Israelis are being told to trade land for peace. Not only for the sake of America's relationships with Syria and Saudi Arabia – which have not lifted their 43-year old declarations of war with the tiny Jewish state – but, primarily for the sake of "Palestinian nationalism." The concept of trading land for peace to fulfill the so-called Palestinian right of self-determination is a ruse. It is a ruse no less than that perpetrated against the Jews when they were marched into what they were told were work camps through gates that proclaimed *"Arbeit Macht Frei."*

It is a ruse because the Palestinians do not want just a piece of Israel. It is a ruse because the Arabs do not give a damn about the Palestinians; they only want to destroy Israel. And it is a ruse because to the rest of the world, save only America, Israel is expendable. Oil comes first.

* * *

What has changed in the last 12 months that Israel should again be compelled to choose between suicide and murder? Only that the belligerent Arab states of Syria, Saudi Arabia, Egypt have exacted the coinage of compromise from the United States in exchange for their cooperation in the Gulf War. Has the Saudi monarchy withdrawn its economic embargo of Israel? No. Has the bellicose Syrian warlord ceased his state of war against the Jewish State? Again, no. Has the dull Jordanian king diluted his enmity against the only democracy in the Middle East? Indeed, not. In fact, he aligned Jordan with Saddam Hussein and lent Jordanian air space to the Iraqis to send missiles into Tel Aviv for no purpose other than the indiscriminate murder of women and children.

Why should the free and faithful Israelis place their trust in Arafat, and, it is also fair to ask, what are the true aspirations of the Palestinian leaders? These are, to be sure, fair questions that the world should be asking before it demands substantial concessions from the Jewish state, which has lived in a state of military alert since its birth.

Arafat has issued a declaration that he alone must approve the Palestinians appointed to sit down at an international peace conference with the Israelis. Imagine Israel negotiating for her life with a line-up of Arafat clones. This from the man who fancies himself the president of a free and democratic Arab Palestine.

Is it of no consequence that Arafat spills Jewish blood with zeal and undisguised delight? Lest we forget, Arafat's prime targets are not the soldiers and military installations. Rather, they are civilians, women and children, tourists, people on buses, the man in the street.

Is it of no consequence that Arafat's PLO is still constitutionally dedicated to the destruction of Israel? Is it of no consequence that the PLO funded and organized the slaughter of Israeli athletes at the Munich Olympics, the massacre of tourists on the Haifa-Tel Aviv coastal road and, God help us, the murder of 21 children in their schoolhouse in Ma'alot? Is it of no consequence that he has publicly renounced terrorism for political expediency only to soil persistently his hands with the blood of Jewish innocents? And is it of no consequence that he has had murdered over 440 brother Palestinians whom he merely suspected of "collaboration" with Israel?

* * *

And what of the Palestinians themselves? It should be troubling to us that the men they have de facto designated to lead and represent them are dedicated, not to peace, but to annihilation of the Jewish state and every Jew within it. It should be troubling to us that when Iraq went to war over Kuwait, the Palestinians cast their lot with Saddam Hussein. It should be troubling to us that when Iraq sent Scud missiles into Israel the Palestinians stood on their rooftops and cheered. It should be troubling to us that the Palestinians do not want just the West Bank; they want all of Israel, and they want it to be, to take a phrase from one of Arafat's heroes, *Judenrein*.

It should be troubling that if seven months ago the West

Bank had been under Palestinian control, Scud missiles could have landed in Tel Aviv, Haifa and the Galilee in mere seconds, and Saddam Hussein's army would have been perched on Israel's border needing to negotiate a mere 10-mile march to cut Israel in half. Palestinian armies would have been fighting in Jerusalem, and destroying synagogues and Jewish cemeteries just as Jordan did when it controlled the West Bank and East Jerusalem between 1949 and 1967.

* * *

Moreover, if the rest of the world gave to the concept of self-determination the same coinage elsewhere as it does where Israel is concerned, it would have sued for peace globally: North Korea would have yielded to South Korea, Russia would have been forced to abandon the Baltic States it purchased from Hitler, China would be expelled from Tibet, etc. Syria's de facto annexation of Lebanon would be declared null and void. The Kurds would have their own homeland, the Spanish Basques theirs, and the Sunni and Shiite theirs, too. Is this a matter of principle or merely a question of whose ox is being gored?

* * *

Are we now to believe that Arafat is the man in whom the Israelis should repose their confidence and future? Dare we force Israel to place in his hands her national security and the lives of her children? Must Israel carve from its already precarious borders an independent state from which the Palestinians and Arab armies are further enabled to conduct a perpetual war of "liberation?" The concept of self-determination, though not by any means an absolute right, has some validity. But its proclamation lies foul in the mouth of those who would use it as a pretext for tyranny and genocide.

August 8, 1991

What You Wish For

"Some rise by sin; others by virtue fall."
— *Measure for Measure*, Act II, Scene I

From at least as far back as the legend of King Midas, we have been warned: "Be careful what you wish for. You may get it." Time and again, we have failed to heed the Greek chorus and we could almost hear them laughing in the background, "We told you so."

It is entirely likely that we are now at another such moment in history. The American president is embarked upon a noble crusade: democratization. The Palestinian Arabs may again go to the polls; this time to elect parliamentary and municipal representatives. We have encouraged this. Representative government is as mother's milk to Americans.

The problem is that democratic elections do not necessarily portend freedom. Reliable polls indicate that Hamas and other terrorists will emerge victorious in many of those free elections. Even if they fail to garner a majority, it is likely they will be elected in so large a number that Mr. Abbas and Fatah may very well be forced to give them "a seat at the table" and perhaps even a place in a coalition government. Should that happen, Israel will be forced onto the horns of a dilemma. It will be demanded that Israel negotiate its future with a democratically elected government comprised of people dedicated to her destruction. The historical Arab demand that the Jewish state die by murder or suicide will no longer involve a choice.

While we are celebrating – perhaps prematurely – democracy's victories in Iraq, Afghanistan and Lebanon, it would be wise to understand exactly what democratic elections may bring us. Mahmoud Abbas, known by his *nom de guerre* Abu Mazen, did not just spring from a shell like Venus. The man has a past. He has a history. Hailed by the West as a "moderate," he was for decades the adviser and confidant of the late Mr. Arafat and architect of the Palestinian war plan. Among other things, Abbas financed the slaughter of Israel's athletes at the Munich Olympics and organized the hijacking of the *Achille Lauro*, on which a disabled American Jew was shot and thrown into the sea with his wheelchair. No less so than the late Mr. Arafat, Mahmoud Abbas is subtle, false and treacherous, disguised in a suit and a grandfatherly smile. To be sure, there is no evidence that Abbas has undergone a Sadat-like metamorphosis. Rather, there are reasons, both good and many, to doubt whether Mr. Abbas and the Palestinian Authority even want a two-state peace.

Although Mr. Abbas has had months – and a king's ransom in foreign aid – to make changes, he refuses to tackle the sine qua non for advancing the peace process: destruction of the terrorist network. Since the momentous meeting at Sharm el-Sheikh, Hamas, Hizbullah, etc., operate openly and in defiance of his supposed authority and continue to kill Israelis. While many attacks have been prevented by the IDF and the security fence, the Palestinian Authority's so-called security forces have sat on their hands as arms are smuggled into, manufactured in and carried through the streets of Gaza right under their noses.

Hamas, Hizbullah, Islamic Jihad and Fatah's own Al Aksa Martyrs Brigade all know they are free to act as they wish so long as they don't completely muck up the current "cease-fire." They are free to catch their breath and rearm. We have President Abbas, who has repeatedly stated that he will not let the PA's police either fire on Palestinians or disarm the terrorists, to thank for this horrific state of affairs.

President Abbas's plan to deal with the terrorists and released prisoners is ingenious in its simplicity: welcome them into the Palestinian security forces, make them promise in writing not to kill Israelis, and then rearm them. Co-opt the killers rather than confront them. Not content to place the foxes in charge of the chicken coop, Abu Mazen intends to place the foxes directly *in* the chicken coop.

What about the weapons leaking daily through the Egyptian border and manufactured in Gaza? President Abbas has that figured out as well: after the elections, all terrorists will be incorporated into the Palestinian political system, which then will have no need for terrorism, weaponry or, therefore, the terrorist organizations such as Hamas and Islamic Jihad. All weapons, he expects, will be turned in to the state. "When a militia turns into a political party," President Abbas recently opined, "I believe the issue of a need for arms becomes irrelevant.... There will be," he declares, "one authority, one law and one legal gun." (It has a familiar ring to it, no? *Ein Volk, ein Reich, ein Fuhrer!*") As though the way to fight crime were to give guns and badges to the criminals. Hamas promptly issued its own statement that its participation in elections "does not mean it is on the way to becoming a political party" and that it will never disarm. In the meantime, mortars continue to be fired at Israeli settlements in and out of Gaza, and teenage suicide-bombers are sent daily on their missions of death…all under the watchful eyes of the PA security forces. A salutary beginning for a criminal democracy.

Meanwhile, Palestinians are growing disenchanted with Fatah corruption and wildfire anarchy. With Hamas filling the municipal, economic and educational vacuum, its candidates are running strong everywhere. And, as all this unfolds, Abu Mazen's hold on the Palestinian body politic deteriorates.

* * *

If peace is to have even a scintilla of hope, the Palestinian president must take on the terrorists. He must do something to assert his authority and credibility just as Ben Gurion did when he ordered the sinking of the *Altalena*. If Abbas fails to sink his *Altalena*, i.e., eliminate or disarm the terrorists and take command of the inner workings of the political and police functions, he will fall by the wayside as so much background noise.

Almost 70 years ago, on October 5, 1938, upon Neville Chamberlain's return from Munich, the great Churchill addressed the House of Commons. His words now, as then, should unnerve our complacency. He declared the Munich agreement "a total and unmitigated defeat…. The utmost he [Chamberlain] has been able to gain for Czechoslovakia in the matters which were in dispute has been that the German dictator, instead of snatching the victuals from the table, has been content to have them served to him course by course."

Churchill's ability to distinguish between reality and wishful thinking was more inimical to Hitler's Reich than the short distance between Dover and Calais.

Today Israel is being force-fed a Palestinian state in Gaza, and then in Judea and Samaria. As Abu Mazen continues his plan for the staged destruction of Israel – and Hamas prepares its velvet *coup d'état* – Israel must resist the pressure to negotiate for its life with those who insist on her death.

There is no reason to believe that today's Palestinians are less dedicated to Israel's destruction than they were five years ago. The PA's utter failure to deal with the terrorists in any meaningful way cannot be swept under the rug. Appeasement of the Palestinians is regarded as weakness. There is no easy way out of this, and the only way out requires complete destruction of the terrorists.

We should recall yet another of Churchill's observations: "Mr. Chamberlain's government was given to choose between war and shame. It has chosen shame. It will surely have war."

Terrorists have no place in civilized society. Not even if they are freely elected. Listen carefully now. Do you hear the Greeks?

April 22, 2005

Old Wine in Old Bottles

"Why, I can smile, and murder whilst I smile;
And cry "Content!" to that which grieves my heart;
And Frame my face with artificial tears for all occasions...
I can change colors with the chameleons,
Change shapes with Proteus for advantage,
And Like a Sinon take another Troy.
I'll drown more sailors than the mermaids shall,
Deceive more slyly than Ulysses,
And send the murderous Machiavelli to school!
Can I do this and cannot get a crown?
Tut! Were it further off, I'll pluck it down."

3 Henry VI, Act III, Scene II

For the better part of the last two weeks, the Jews of Gaza have gathered their possessions and their dead as they left their homes, schools, synagogues and businesses. Fortunately, confrontations between the settlers and the Israeli police were relatively few and mild. Considering what was being asked of the settlers, their reactions were both very human (distress) and superhuman (non-violent). It could have been much worse – tear gas, rubber bullets, batons, etc. – and anywhere else in the Middle East it would have been so.

The Jewish nation has done something utterly unique: unilateral withdrawal. No *quid pro quo*. The Israeli army has dismantled those synagogues of Gaza capable of being dismantled; those that were not have their holy relics removed and the structures left intact. This was done because Palestinian President Mahmoud Abbas had rejected out of hand Israeli pleas to safeguard Jewish houses of worship. This man Abbas, who seeks international recognition of Gaza's sovereignty – he's not ready to call it Palestine lest that leave the impression that Judea and Samaria are not part of Palestine – who has at his command, if not control, tens of thousands of armed security forces, refused to station any police or soldiers to protect Israel's last remaining holy synagogues – and the last physical evidence of the presence of the Jews.

The Palestinian Authority offered to stand by as its citizens defiled and destroyed Jewish shuls, as Israel engaged in one of the great moral debates of its 57-year history: unilateral disengagement and what to do with the Gaza synagogues. Should Jews have destroyed those synagogues that could not be dismantled or leave them behind and let the Arabs have their way with them? For reasons best left to politicians and Talmudic scholars, Israel decided not to destroy what was left behind. Perhaps the thought of Jews putting a wrecking ball to a holy structure was more than could be borne. And in some eerie way, destruction of the Gaza synagogues could be likened to the suicides at Masada in 73 CE.

There was never so much as a scintilla of hope that the Arabs would respect Jewish holy sites. Knowing full well what the Arabs have done to the enemy dead in centuries past, even the remains of our dead had to be exhumed from Gaza's Jewish cemeteries to be taken back to Israel for their next "final resting place."

In fact, within minutes after the departure of the IDF, four synagogues were torched by Palestinians waving PA and Hamas flags and celebrating with weapons fire. Prominent were hats declaring, "Today Gaza, Tomorrow Jerusalem." Indeed, even before the fires had died and the smoke cleared, the Palestinian president and a senior Hamas official defended destruction of the synagogues. Characteristically, Abbas declared that the Israelis had left no synagogues behind in Gaza; only dilapidated buildings on the brink of collapse. Hamas spokesman Ismail Haniyeh sneered that his people "would not allow any Wailing Walls on our blessed land."

We were not engaged in a mere academic exercise. Israel is being pressed to make huge sacrifices to bring peace to the region with a people who time and again has shown their blind, categorical hatred of the Jews. These are the people to whom Israel is expected to turn over Judea and Samaria and half of Jerusalem;

Israel and the Palestinians – What the Media Aren't Telling You

the people to whom we are to entrust our holy sites in a future Palestine. We know what the Arabs do to our holy sites. The burial place of Joseph, for example, was taken apart stone by stone and rebuilt as a mosque from which Arabs old and young are exhorted to kill Jews. Between 1949 and 1967, the cemeteries of Jerusalem were vandalized and those headstones that weren't shattered were toppled and used as urinals by the Jordanians.

* * *

As all this unfolded, America and the rest of the international community applauded Prime Minister Sharon's "bold initiative" and the sacrifices made by the Israelis to bring about peace. Yet, the unanswered question still hangs in the air like a pestilent congregation of vapors. Why were 1.4 million Arabs unable to live in peace with 8,000 Jews?

America, the United Nations, the so-called Quartet, the European Union all participated in the ethnic cleansing of Gaza. "Get out of Gaza," Sharon was told, "and the world will recognize Israel as a peacemaker." "Get out of Gaza and we'll give you money to relocate the settlers" who made up a less than 1 percent of Gaza's population. How bad could this expulsion be? Almost every country in Europe has at one time or another expelled the Jews, and Gaza is so small and such a tiny geographic sacrifice for peace.

When Abbas demanded the expulsion of every Jew in Gaza – as the Palestinians surely will of every Jew in Judea and Samaria – the United States and the European Union should have spoken in one voice against this apartheid. And had the Palestinians refused, an international embargo of Gaza should have been effected until this racist demand was withdrawn. But, because it was only the Jews – and merely 8,000 of us at that – the world sat on its hands and nodded benignly.

Thus, the Palestinian bargain was: Get every last Jew out of Gaza and then we can get the peace process on track to deal with the issues of final borders, Jerusalem and the "refugees." It is the same old Palestinian game: get everything they want and then sit down and lie about what they will do for Israel. It's been stated so frequently now that only the intellectually anesthetized or disabled fail to see the Palestinian design for the staged destruction of all Israel.

* * *

The whole business of disengagement should not have been necessary; but it was, owing to global anti-Semitism. Too many calamities have befallen our people because each horror was preceded by the casual rationalization, "It's only the Jews."

Before the Taliban destroyed the 800-year old Buddhas in Afghanistan, the international community from presidents and prime ministers to the pope himself pleaded with them not to do it. Yet, no one outside of Israel spoke out to save our synagogues.

When Muslims were being ethnically cleansed from Central Europe, the international community intervened with force. But when the Palestinians demanded that every Jew be expelled from Gaza, not a voice was raised in protest.

When the Huns destroyed the 13th Battalion of the Roman army, an entire empire mourned. But when the Third Reich came to destroy all the Jews of Europe, not even the great democracies of England and America so much as lifted a finger to help save the People of the Book. No concentration camps were bombed; not 10 meters of railroad track were destroyed.

When terrorism struck the 1972 Olympics in Munich, Avery Brundage, head of the IOC, stopped the games for only one day and ordered the Olympics to continue…and every nation stayed and participated, except the Israelis who went home to bury their dead.

When 300 Chechan children were murdered, the world stopped to express its collective horror and sympathy. News stories were broadcast, newspapers condemned it and talking heads opined on the savagery of the terrorists. Yet in 1974, when 21 children were murdered in the schoolhouse in Ma'alot by Palestinian terrorists disguised in IDF uniforms, nary an eyebrow was raised.

When a suicide-bomber killed an emergency room doctor and his daughter having coffee and a tender moment together on the eve of her wedding, the Palestinians celebrated by handing out candy; but not a single United Nations resolution was even offered to condemn the cold-blooded murder.

As murders, tragedies and efforts to delegitimize the Jewish state piled on, little was offered other than condemnation of a so-called "occupation" created solely by the Palestinian refusal to stop killing Jews.

* * *

The international community is barely beginning to understand what is at stake: Western civilization itself, the Enlightenment and the Renaissance. So it was that the terrorists observed and remembered that Western Civilization sat on its hands when grim-visaged death came for the Jews. Now the people of London, New York, Madrid, Kenya and Beslan have had terrorism forced down their throats. But this is only because with every unanswered attack on Israelis the terrorists have grown in confidence, strength and support. Terroristic murder is not over with. Not by a long shot.

And the Palestinians? Unwilling either to seize another opportunity to bring peace to their culture of death, or to relinquish their goal of destroying all of Israel, this war, the intifada, pauses only to catch its breath. Palestinian mothers will blow themselves up and parents will bury their children. Will the Palestinians, as Abba Eban used to say, continue to "miss every opportunity to miss an opportunity?" Of course. Because the only opportunity they are interested in seizing is for complete control and sovereignty over what they call "Palestine, from the river to the sea."

That is their objective and why this is a war to the death. To the Palestinians, the only opportunity that matters is the one that places Israel's neck on the chopping block.

It is important to note that when Palestinians kill Jews, President Abbas condemns the murders only because it does not advance the Palestinian cause. Not, mind you, because murder is wrong; only that it hurts their image and public relations program.

Finally, each Palestinian assurance of peaceful intentions lies rotting in the cesspool of meaningless and empty past promises. The Israelis will do well not to trust their sugared words, for the Palestinians are all of them so steeped in blood that sin shall pluck on sin.

September 12, 2005

Judenrein in the Promised Land

As the Annapolis Conference rightfully fades into oblivion, US Secretary of State Condoleezza Rice, Israeli Prime Minister Ehud Olmert and PA President Mahmoud Abbas have returned home with an American mission, indeed, a presidential injunction, in hand: Make peace before President Bush leaves office. The impediments to a two-state solution are multiple and complex. Sisyphean to say the least. Aside from core issues such as refugees, borders and Jerusalem, there is another issue tied to the "settlers" question that seems to have eluded almost everyone: Why must the Jews leave Judea and Samaria?

We are made to agonize over the Palestinian demand that the settlers be removed and struggle to define the terms under which they may stay where they are. Expansion by "natural growth," contiguity, borders and other issues may be solved by negotiation if the parties are so inclined. But the question that continues to nag is why every last Jew cannot live in peace in what may become Palestine.

The Left, Center, and even elements of the Right insist that in the name of achieving peace, at long last, the settlements must go. It is the price the Israelis have to pay to get the Palestinians to love us, or at least stop killing us.

Many remain skeptical, at best, that a two-state peace is achievable. But of all the impediments that must be overcome, it seems that the presence of Jews in a Palestine is one of the concerns that is most easily addressed. And of all the mistakes Israel can make in yielding to Palestinian demands, perhaps the mistake most easy to avoid is the Palestinian demand that the settlers have to return to Israel. The question that must be asked is why the dejudaization of Judea and Samaria is a condition for peace.

* * *

The concept of land for peace has a long and generally undistinguished history. The most prominent, and perhaps only, success story is the Israeli decision to remove its settlers from the Sinai in order to reach a peace agreement with Egypt. While offered by the "peace camp" as solid precedent, the circumstances are so disparate as to make the analogy dangerously attractive. First, we were dealing with two sovereign states. Second, there was no dispute about what specific land was involved. Third, and perhaps most relevant, there were two leaders who had the power and authority to speak for their countries. Today, we are told to make peace with a quasi-government which lacks a defined land and, significantly, is incapable of dealing with a geographically and politically separated population, at least half of which is at odds with President Abbas, the nominal head of Fatah's West Bank Palestinians.

Abbas lacks both credibility and authority. It is uncertain for whom he speaks and it is extremely doubtful that he has the authority to make an agreement with Israel and the power to make it stick. And that is just in the West Bank. It is beyond peradventure that Abbas could not organize a parade in Gaza; it remains to be seen if he can even show his face there.

Sadat, on the other hand, was recognized and empowered within his country as its leader. He more or less had the support of the people and, not to be overlooked, the military. His assassination notwithstanding, the Camp David Accords remain the law of the land, even if we are left with a blistering cold peace today.

Thus, in the Palestinian context, the historical use of Israel's removal of its settlers from the Sinai as a useful precedent stands on the thinnest of ice.

* * *

Just as the creation of a Palestinian state in Judea and Samaria is supposed to bring Israel peace and security, so was it with the disengagement from Gaza, which failed on a number of levels, not the least of which was that Gaza predictably became a terrorist entity. But, beyond mere disengagement, the Palestinians demanded – backed by Israeli, American and European complicity – that every last one of the settlers be removed. Round and round we debated the security consequences and whether the Gazans had the ability and desire to turn this small strip on the Mediterranean into a working democracy, or at least a quasi-democracy with a viable economy. Everything was done to make them succeed, and hundreds of millions of dollars were placed at their disposal. But the Gaza experiment has failed, and even as the last Jews departed, the remaining synagogues were burned to the ground. As Gaza's Hamas leader Haniyeh scoffed, "We don't want any Wailing Walls on our land." And Abbas, the moderate, asked "What synagogues?"

What happened that it was necessary to make Gaza *Judenrein*? Stripped of embellishments, sophistry and politically correct analyses, the disengagement was necessary because 1.4 million Palestinians refused to live in peace with 8,000 Jews. That is what the disengagement was about. Jews. Were it otherwise, Hamas would not still be shelling Sderot and Ashkelon, cities *inside* the Green Line. If retreat behind the Green Line were truly their objection, then these two cities would have been left in peace. One would think that Gaza had laid to rest forever the "land for peace" canard that the Left has persuaded itself is a fair and reasonable expectation. The daily barrage of rockets and mortars show that this conflict is not about land, but about Jews.

* * *

The Palestinians – indeed, almost everyone – accuse Israel of practicing apartheid. Even Prime Minister Olmert has opined that unless the Palestinians are given their own state, it will inevitably lead Israel to become a nation practicing apartheid. This is, to be sure, a false and reckless assertion; another arrow in the quiver of the Palestinians. And the fact that it issued from Israel's leader gives substance to the ludicrous Palestinian charge of apartheid.

The removal of the Jews of Gaza was not an act of apartheid, which is the enforced separation of races, or in this case, religions. Apartheid would have permitted Gaza's 8,000 Jewish settlers to remain in Gaza in their little Bantustans, separate and apart from their Palestinian neighbors. But the Jews were not permitted to stay in Gaza, even under a policy of strict apartheid. Instead, the Palestinians demanded the expulsion of every last Jew in Gaza. To the list of countries that have expelled the Jews – such as England, France and Spain – in 2005 we added Gaza. In a sickeningly familiar scene, the Jews of Gaza – with their families, possessions, religious books and artifacts and, even their dead – were organized and led out of that tiny strip of land in yet another expulsion. Knowing how the Arabs had treated Jewish graves in the past, it became necessary for Gaza's Jews to remove their deceased loved ones, and carry them to their next "final" resting place.

The tragedy of Gaza was aggravated by the fact that it was supported by Europe and the United States. Sharon was urged to play the peacemaker and was assured that Israel would earn vast capital in the form of worldwide approval and assistance. Yielding Gaza, he was told, would mostly free up the IDF's Southern Command. For the sake of peace, the Jews of Gaza should cooperate in yet another expulsion, but what followed was not peace. It was escalation.

* * *

Now history is looking to repeat itself in Judea and Samaria, the cradle of the Jewish people and our most historically significant land. And once again we are asked to believe that this expulsion – the last territorial demand of the Arabs? – from our biblical homeland will bring us that very peace and acceptance for which we have waited in vain since our first expulsion.

Messrs. Bush and Olmert, arm in arm with Mesdames Rice and Livni, again stand behind Israel at the precipice urging us forward yet again. The Palestinians have already told us that they will not tolerate any Jews in "their" homeland. In fact, only this past January, a PA spokesman assured us that they would not lift a finger to protect any Jews remaining in Judea and Samaria. The West Bank Jews will be on their own and beyond the jurisdiction of the IDF.

The Palestinians are preparing a huge sign for their new

border: "NO JEWS!" and once again our leaders are urging us to accept this naked expression of Jew-hatred. And again the Americans and Europeans are standing there prepared to lead us out of the promised land; all without objection as though it were as natural the setting of the sun.

The only issues given to discussion have been about security matters, to be sure, of paramount importance. But, why has no one questioned the ethics or morality of demanding that Judea and Samaria be *Judenrein*? I don't expect to hear objections from *The New York Times*, CNN, the BBC, *Le Monde*, *La República* or Reuters. But where are the voices of the Israelis? Why would the editor of *Ha'aretz*, rather than see his country flourish, ask the American secretary of state to have it "raped"? Why didn't the prime minister, or at least the leaders of Likud or Yisrael Beiteinu, not demand an explanation for why Jews cannot live in peace in a Palestinian state – or anywhere else, for that matter.

And what has seized the throat of Diaspora Jewry? Fears of rocking the boat? Accusations of divided loyalty? The thought of assimilation brought to naught? From the comfort of our vacation homes, driving foreign cars, and spending a small fortune to send our children to Ivy League universities, too many have forgotten what our 19th- and early 20th-century forebears had to learn from their suffering: what it meant to be a Jew before there was an Israel. Far from the shtetls, pogroms and the humiliation of expulsions, few in the Diaspora are willing to test their Zionism, much less to stand up as Jews against anti-Semitism. It appears to be lost on our fellow Jews in the Diaspora that we have a stake in protecting Israel. If we don't, how can we expect anyone else to care?.

Proponents of the two-state solution are in pain over the "rightness" of the "occupation" – made necessary by Palestinian terrorism – but fail to explain why religious cleansing is right. The morality of the "occupation" seems to have been measured in terms of utopia rather than in the context of a nation at war and in which her civilians are primary targets. Such proponents should spend the weekend in Sderot and ponder there the "rightness" of withdrawing the IDF to inside the Green Line. It hardly needs pointing out that the armistice boundaries are not an impediment to Palestinian terror. Surely, it is clear that the IDF's presence in Judea and Samaria is the only thing standing between Abbas and a Hamas takeover of what is left of the PA. If the IDF pulls out of Judea and Samaria, Hamas will take control there quicker than you can say Rafik Hariri.

* * *

If it is appropriate, or "right," for the Jews of Judea and Samaria to be expelled from their homes, where they live peacefully, should not one also be able to ask whether the Israelis should be allowed to expel all Arabs from Israel? If we are compelled to accept the Palestinian position that people may be expelled strictly on the basis of religion, then all other considerations – moral, ethical, legal, rational, etc. – become irrelevant. It all turns, not on principle, but on whose ox is gored. Sauce for the goose, perhaps? However, not to paint with too broad a brush, would it not be entirely logical and fair to expel any Palestinians who engage in terrorism, or who urge the destruction of Israel, or provide aid and comfort to those who do? Under such circumstances, the expulsion of an Israeli-Arab would be a legitimate exercise of the right of self-defense, not to mention being an appropriate enforcement of the rule of law.

Needless to say, it would be immoral for Israel to do to the Palestinians what they demand of the Jews. But, if that's the case, where are the voices of reason demanding protection for the Jews in Judea and Samaria, or elsewhere in Arabia? The fact is that Israel is held to, and often exceeds, a standard much higher than that expected of Arab countries, or indeed any other.

It is inescapable that the demand to remove the settlers is motivated by anti-Semitism, pure and simple. This conflict is not about borders. It is not about Palestinian rights or Palestinian autonomy. It is not even about Palestinian nationalism. It is about Jews.

We should reflect on the American experience with slavery

and segregation. The defeated states of the Confederacy did not agree to rejoin the Union on the condition that blacks would remain slaves. Sixty years ago, African-Americans were not told to "deal with it" to keep the peace. James Meredith was not told to forget about going to college at "Ole Miss" so there could be peace and calm instead of riots. It got ugly and it got violent, but the right of all Americans to attend any college, and by extension to live anywhere, was vindicated. These are human rights, and cannot be bartered, even to preserve a perverted peace. Peace at the price of dignity is too high for anyone to have to pay.

* * *

Removal of the settlers is not what some call "pragmatic Zionism." Historically, it is true that Ben Gurion decided that half a loaf was better than none, and if pushed against that same wall today, we would support him in making the same decision. But the issue of the settlers is not about creating borders and carving up land. It is the principle of *Judenrein*, which has caused us to be a people without a land for millennia; a principle that dictates that Jews – wherever we may be – are guests in someone else's home. As history has also taught us, when push comes to shove, guests may be expelled, or murdered. Pragmatism will only take us so far.

* * *

The anti-settler coalition decries the loss of the "essential rightness of our cause." To what cause are they referring? The right of Israel to exist? No, I believe they are referring to our right to live in peace. But, the right to live in peace cannot be so narrowly construed geographically as to apply only to pre-1967 Israel. Why should Jews not be allowed to live in peace in Palestine? Anywhere? That, too, is the rightness of our cause.

If the most important proof in the arsenal of our enemies is the settlements, then the Palestinians must be compelled to convince us, in the most lucid, rational, ethical and moral terms, why the mere presence of Jews is so toxic as to demand our eternal quarantine. Jews in Judea and Samaria are not stealing the land and livelihoods of our neighbors. There is enough room there among 1.5 million Palestinians for 250,000 Jews. What an absurdity it is to claim that a Jewish family living on a farm deprives a Palestinian of his "life, liberty and the pursuit of happiness."

* * *

Even among the supporters of Prime Minister Olmert, there is at least some acknowledgment that withdrawing from the settlements will not appease our enemies and, therefore, Israel should not leave unilaterally, without guarantees, safeguards and milestones. The problem is that there are no guarantees or promises which the Palestinians can make that are credible. The Palestinians have lied their way past the Israelis ever since Oslo. One after another, Palestinian promises lie rotting next to one another. Israelis out jogging in the hills are murdered by the Palestinian security forces, which America insists be trained and well-armed; the same security forces that attempted to assassinate Prime Minister Olmert on his way to Ramallah for a meeting with Abbas. Yet Olmert imbues Abbas and his corrupt gangsters with honor and trust, creating their bona fides out of thin air. That Olmert believes that Abbas is a man of peace is tragic and his refusal to deal with reality is consistent with one who is unable to distinguish spit from rain.

The Palestinians have failed to make any substantive effort to live in peace with the Israelis. To this very day, the official Palestinian media, which remain controlled by Abbas, continue to spew an unbroken stream of anti-Israel and anti-Semitic venom. It is worth noting that upon the recent death of master terrorist George Habash, President Abbas ordered all Palestinian flags lowered to half-mast for three days in recognition of the "great loss for the Palestinian cause and the Palestinians people for whom he fought for 60 years." There is no end to the incitement, and there is no reason to believe it will ever end.

Gaza has taught us well that appeasement does not work. It

is a sign of weakness in the Arab world, to be met with increased hostility and violence. Olmert only encourages Palestinian terrorism and obduracy when he says that he is "tired of fighting, we are tired of being courageous, we are tired of winning, we are tired of defeating our enemies, we want to be able to live in an entirely different environment of relations with our enemies." Olmert could offer Abbas *all* of Israel except Dizengoff Center and that would still not suffice. I am reminded of Churchill's comment upon Chamberlain's return from Munich: "The prime minister was given to choose between war and shame. He has chosen shame. He will surely have war." The Middle East is a venue of continuous war with only interstitial moments of calm.

The Palestinians continue to take all and give nothing. They are given prisoners, money, electricity, fuel, checkpoints closed, and roadblocks lifted, all *gratis*; and then Israel obsequiously yields more and more to prop up a hopeless Abbas. And Israel remains on the receiving end of non-stop incitement and terrorism. Like a dysfunctional 3-year-old who puts her hand on the hot stove again and again, Israel's leaders seem incapable of learning from experience.

If 3,000 years of wars and expulsions have not adequately taught us not put our hands on a hot stove again, Israel will continue to feed the beast that demands our expulsion and extinction.

February 8, 2008